Dirty Work

Dirty Work

Immigrants in Domestic Service, Agriculture, and Prostitution in Sicily

Jeffrey E. Cole and Sally S. Booth

LEXINGTON BOOKS

A division of
ROWMAN & LITTLEFIELD PUBLISHERS, INC.
Lanham • Boulder • New York • Toronto • Plymouth, UK

LEXINGTON BOOKS

A division of Rowman & Littlefield Publishers, Inc.
A wholly owned subsidiary of The Rowman & Littlefield Publishing Group, Inc.
4501 Forbes Boulevard, Suite 200
Lanham, MD 20706

Estover Road
Plymouth PL6 7PY
United Kingdom

British Library Cataloguing in Publication Information Available

Library of Congress Cataloging-in-Publication Data

Cole, Jeffrey, 1958–
  Dirty work : immigrants in domestic service, agriculture, and
prostitution in Sicily / Jeffrey E. Cole and Sally S. Booth.
      p. cm.
  Includes bibliographical references and index.
  ISBN-13: 978-0-7391-1723-1 (cloth : alk. paper)
  ISBN-10: 0-7391-1723-8 (cloth : alk. paper)
  ISBN-13: 978-0-7391-1724-8 (pbk. : alk. paper)
  ISBN-10: 0-7391-1724-6 (pbk. : alk. paper)
  1. Alien labor—Italy—Sicily. 2. Women alien labor—Italy—Sicily. I. Booth,
Sally S., 1959– II. Title.
  HD8488.A2C66 2007
  331.6′209458—dc22   2006030820

Printed in the United States of America

⊚™ The paper used in this publication meets the minimum requirements of
American National Standard for Information Sciences—Permanence of Paper for
Printed Library Materials, ANSI/NISO Z39.48–1992.

Contents

Acknowledgments

In the course of researching and writing this book (1998–2006), we have benefited from the assistance and encouragement of many institutions and individuals. The project was set into motion by Russell King's invitation to contribute to an issue of *Modern Italy* devoted to immigration. Michael Blim, Tony Galt, David Kertzer, Winnie Lem, Andrew Lyons, George Saunders, Peter Schneider, and Tom Wilson have all given us sage advice on conference presentations and article manuscripts. At different times, Edward Fischer and Jane Schneider read the manuscript in its entirety and offered excellent advice, as did anonymous reviewers. At Lexington, the path to publication was smoothed by Serena Krombach and Kathryn Holmes.

In Italy, we marveled at the willingness of Italians and immigrants alike to field our innumerable questions and assist us with a thousand and one practical dilemmas. They interrupted their busy schedules to describe the immigrant experience in Sicily. They gave us tours of their neighbors, introduced us to friends and potential research contacts, and shared their stories and aspirations. They welcomed us into their homes, fed us, and taught us how to cook Sicilian, Ghanaian, Filipino, and other cuisines. In Palermo, we remember Ambi, Naser, Daniele Costantino, Renata D'Aietti, Antonio Fioravante, Desmond Folayan, Tiziana Gulotta, Vincenzo Guarrasi, Regina Hagan, Fateh Hamdan, Franco La Cecla, Rosaria Maida, Fabrizio Mangione, Don Badassare Meli, Beatrice Monroy, Islam M., Marilou, Ernesto Nauaratnam, Emmanuel Nebafuh, Nicodemos, Sirus Nikoo, Bolyvie S., Guilia de Spuches, Abu Suhel, Giampiero Valenti, and Zine. We had the pleasure to meet with representatives of many institutions as well: Gaia Colombo

(Arcidonna), Shelley Cavalieri and Vivian Wiwolokie (Associazione Pelle-grino della Terra), Caterina LoCastro (Caritas), Alfonso Manocchio (CEMI), Cettina Di Benedetto (Centro Sociale Sant'Anna), Barbara Gardinello and Lamia (Centro Cooperazione Sud-Sud), Salvatore LoBalbo (CGIL), Ar-mondo Volpin (CISL-ANOLF), Ilaria Sposito and Totó (La Falene), Ida Agosta and Teresa Cirivello (INEA), Vittoria Messina (Le Onde), and Ninni Amari, Bibi, J.C., and Marianna Di Rosa (Progetto). In Mazara del Vallo, we enjoyed meeting Mario Foderà (GCIL) and Eva Carlestål on immigrant mat-ters. In Vittoria and Santa Croce Camerina, we count ourselves fortunate to have met Abdelkrim Boufermes, Francesca Campanella, Eduardo Falla, Lina Di Martino, Guiseppe Miccichè, Antonio Riva, Saoussen M'Saddak, Don Beniamino Sacco, and Slah. In the southeast we also learned much from institutional representatives and members of local government, including Vincenzo La Monica (Caritas), Salvo Cinnirella, Giovanni Consolino, and Giovanni Formica (City of Vittoria), Paolo Aquila and Rhouma Sami (CGIL), and R. Bocchieri and Franco Sisono (CISL). And in Calolziocorte in the far north of Italy, we enjoyed many conversations with Alexis, Apollinaire, Philippe, Jean Roche Toti, Emmanuel Sokouri, and their families.

We happily acknowledge a special debt to our hosts and guides. Pasquale Marchese has always made us feel at home in Sicily. His interest in our project, deft hand in the kitchen, and deep knowledge of Sicily have sustained us during long seasons of fieldwork, as have the wonders of the old mill in Borgetto. When our children, Sam and Jocelyn, think of Sicily, their thoughts and hearts run swiftly to *il mulino* and the attentions of Pasquale, his son Vincenzo, and Elena Paparcone. Our stays in Palermo were made a pleasure thanks to Vincenzo Ognibene and Ina Abbadessa, who opened up their house to us; seeing Vincenzo's studio, savoring his tomato salad, and hearing his peerless and piquant social commentary re-main deeply satisfying. When we remember Palermo, our thoughts al-ways turn to our dear friend, Farah Meija; we have shared many a mem-orable meal, and in so many ways our project is indebted to her vast knowledge of the immigrant situation and extensive contacts. Rosario Lentini's grasp of Sicilian history is matched only by his warmth; we have come to appreciate the island in his company and that of his family. Mary Taylor Simeti and her family gave us a place at the table, sound ideas, and key logistical support in the form of child minding. In Mazara del Vallo, Antonio Cusumano and Karim Hannachi offered us hospitality and the benefit of their own researches. Bartolo Scillieri, in Santa Croce Camerina, has proven a peerless guide to immigration; we admire his dedication and hard work on behalf of Caritas and the Itaca Sud project. We are pro-foundly grateful to Lino Di Rosa, in Vittoria, for making many wonderful things happen. In Calolziocorte, Serikpa Djessi made sure we had a mem-orable time and introduced us to fellow Ivorians who had relocated to northern Italy from Palermo. And in Genova, Emilia Chini arranged appointments and housing, showed us a swell time, and made a compelling argument for our conducting a comparative study in that port city.

The research on which this book is based was supported by a grant from the Wenner-Gren Foundation for Anthropological Research. Released time from Dowling College enabled Cole to devote additional time to writing, and travel and research funds helped defray some of the costs of trips to Sicily. Support from Dowling College (Cole) and Ross School (Booth) enabled us both to present preliminary findings at a number of conferences. With gratitude we acknowledge these sources of financial and institutional support.

We also thank the *Journal of Modern Italian Studies* and *Anthropologica*. Parts of chapter 3 appeared in our "Domestic Work, Family Life, and Immigration," *Journal of Modern Italian Studies* 11, no. 1 (2006): 22–36. Parts of chapter 5 appeared in Cole's "Reducing the Damage: Dilemmas of Anti-Trafficking Efforts among Nigerian Prostitutes in Palermo," *Anthropologica* 48, no. 2 (2006): 217–228.

Maps

Photographs

1

Introduction

Dirty Work explores the causes and consequences of recent immigration to the southern Italian region of Sicily. With its history of massive emigration and anemic economy, Sicily would appear an unlikely destination for tens of thousands of Tunisians, Bangladeshis, Filipinos, Nigerians, Sri Lankans, and others. Yet over the past thirty years foreigners have readily found employment in the island's cities and countryside as Sicilian employers have sought cheap labor and as Sicilians themselves have rejected degrading, dead-end, and low-paying jobs in homes, fields, and streets. Newcomers, often with precarious legal status and desperate to support themselves and their families back home, accept such dirty work as shepherds, fishermen, maids, and field hands. In what has become a well-established pattern, once immigrants receive legal status through one of Italy's periodic amnesty programs, they move from Sicily to the factories and cities of the Italian north, if not beyond, following the same path taken by so many Sicilian emigrants before them.

This book examines the lives and times of immigrants involved in three kinds of dirty work—domestic service, street prostitution, and agriculture. In each of the three case studies we chart the recent history of the relevant sector and explore the participation of foreigners in it. We describe the development of racial and ethnic identity within the crucible of local economy and culture; explore how networks and families promote, guide, and stymie the projects of individuals; and record the occupational and geographical mobility so characteristic of immigrants in Sicily. The rising fortunes of Italy and surging global migration have introduced Sicilians to a very diverse population of foreigners and brought them into contact in unanticipated ways. Throughout the book we seek to capture the dynamic effects of newcomers on Sicilian society and culture and to explore the island's changing relationship to the wider world.

Even a glance at the evening news or our own wardrobe reminds us that the world is connected by an international movement of ideas, goods, services, and people. Immigrants do enjoy financial and professional success in their adopted homelands. But like Haitian men cutting sugar cane in the Dominican Republic, Filipina maids in Singapore, and Chinese peasant girls in Thai brothels, the majority of the world's nearly two hundred million immigrants have been consigned by accident of birth to the dirtiest tasks.[1] Immigrants are commonly thought to pose a danger to host societies, and while newcomers can represent undesirable change there is no denying that they and their families in fact subsidize the families, businesses, and lifestyles of many in economically developed countries. For those living in immigrant destinations, the Sicilian case raises disturbing questions about globalization, the nature of our society, and the hidden foundations of our material comfort. Drawing on observation and discussions with immigrants and Sicilians conducted 1998–2004, we probe the connections—some hidden, others brutally plain—that bind us to others and other lands.

AUGUSTINE'S STORY

On July 16, 1998, we met with Augustine, a twenty-eight-year-old from the Ivory Coast. We had met him days before at a sparsely attended meeting of a short-lived anti-racist association. As we walked from the central train station in Palermo to the apartment he shared with three fellow Ivorians, he gestured toward Sicilian passersby. "They are poor but proud," he smiled. "See how they carry themselves like kings!" His trips to the north had brought him into contact with another kind of Italian—closed and unhappy though economically secure. The contrast occupied his thoughts because, after nearly seven years, he was about to leave this southern city he had come to call home. He had recently quit his job at a health club in Palermo and would soon settle in northeastern Italy, where he expected to find the security of stable employment in a factory.

In the course of the next four hours Augustine poured out his story, describing the hard times of his early years in Sicily, the strain of telling parents that he had no money to send home, the stymied aspirations of social mobility, and the good times, too. Like many other newcomers, he had been drawn to Italy by the country's string of recent amnesty programs and by ease of entry relative to traditional destinations like France. In 1991, he flew to Palermo, becoming part of a growing contingent of

Ghanaians, Ivorians, and others settling in the *centro storico*, the run-down historic city center. He scraped by on occasional work, the generosity of friends and co-nationals, and temporary lodging and other assistance provided by Santa Chiara, a Catholic Church social center serving immigrants and local poor. When his tourist visa expired, Augustine became a *clandestino*, an unauthorized alien. Fearful of any kind of trouble that could lead to deportation, he paid bills on time, avoided police, and walked away from the taunts, rude stares, and thrown food that he encountered in the poorer areas of the city. With time, relations with Sicilians in the old city improved, not least because the West Africans who resided there proved themselves to be good workers and valuable customers.

Augustine enjoyed the vivacious outdoor life of Palermo and appreciated the extroverted and expressive social character of its inhabitants. Unlike most immigrants who socialize primarily with co-nationals, Augustine participated in associational life and counted Sicilians and newcomers of diverse origins among his friends. But he still bridled at the lack of respect shown immigrants and smarted at the exploitation they experienced at the hands of Sicilian employers. The slights to ego, pocketbook, and future security had been many. His Sicilian landlord, who enjoyed visiting the Ivory Coast as a sex tourist, had failed to make promised repairs despite raising the rent several times. When Augustine ventured into a café, the toilet was always "broken," though he noticed Sicilian customers making free use of it. Shop-owners addressed him with the familiar "What do you want" rather than the polite "What would you like, sir?" Employers preferred to hire him under the table, winking and saying how they were going to cheat "Rome"—the central government— out of taxes. Augustine objected to this logic. "They're robbing me of my future," he said, referring to the consequences of not having contributions made in his name to the national social security system. According to Augustine, Sicilians refuse to recognize immigrant contributions even as they relegate foreigners to menial jobs. Said Augustine, "We clean floors, we clean the shit off the bottoms of their old folks. Then they treat us badly, give us no respect because we're dirty! But how can we remain clean doing dirty work?"

To support himself, Augustine had worked as a porter in one of the city's ancient, open-air markets, he had hawked goods along the beaches outside the city, and he had cleaned houses and cared for elderly Sicilians. Twice he joined fellow Ivorians and participated in the tomato harvest in the southern Italian region of Puglia. A recognized symbol of immigrant exploitation, the harvest involves long hours under a relentless summer sun for low pay, the thinly veiled hostility of local residents, routine police raids, and miserable living conditions. One year he narrowly escaped a raid, which netted among others a co-national to whom he had paid a small sum for transportation to and from the fields. Later, taking in the television and newspaper accounts of the incident, Augustine was appalled to find the man referred to as the *capo dei capi neri* ("the boss of the black bosses"). The use of terms reserved for organized crime figures implied that the plight of immigrant laborers was the product of African delinquency rather than the fruit of a silent duplicity cultivated by Italian police, farmers, and politicians. "They treat us like dirt but it's thanks to us that the Italians eat their *spaghetti al pomodoro* [spaghetti with tomato sauce] all year," he observed bitterly. He would never return to the tomato harvest. In 1997 he received his permit, thanks to the amnesty offered under the "Dini" decree (1995). With this in hand, he felt he could escape the insecurity of Palermo's economy. While keenly aware of the rigors of settling in the north, Augustine accepted the challenge with the confidence that he would find documented employment there.

We never saw Augustine again. The next year a mutual Sicilian friend confirmed his account and said he had settled in the Milan area. We have been drawn back time and again to his story, delivered around a kitchen table decorated with plastic flowers. Over the past six years we have often encountered these stories—the simultaneous exasperation with and fondness for Sicily, the path from lapsed tourist visa to authorized residence, the thankless toil in fields and houses, the appetite among Italians for bought sex with Africans, the dangers and stresses of a tenuous existence in a strange land, the frustrating inability to provide for family back home, and immigrant mobility and the inexorable pull of the north. These themes have been repeated in the course of the dozens of interviews conducted with men and women from Africa, Asia, the Middle East, and Latin America.

DIRTY WORK

The common thread of these discussions, and the principal subject of this book, is work. From the holistic perspective of cultural anthropology, the investigation of work offers a sweeping perspective onto the immigrant experience. Virtually all immigrants leave their homes in Africa, Asia, and other parts with the intention of earning money abroad to achieve or maintain economic well-being back at home. Once in Sicily, the character of their days and future prospects are linked to the contours of local economies, employer-employee relations, and emerging ethnic and racial identities and stereotypes. As Augustine's narrative suggests, issues of respect, legality, and exploitation all come into sharp relief at work. His story also points to the northward trajectory so common among those who have obtained their permits. Consideration of a sizable foreign population on an island best known for sending its sons and daughters out into the world also points to continuities and changes in Sicily's participation in a global economy.

In Sicily, immigrants perform all kinds of jobs. A partial list of occupations would include street hawker, window washer, prostitute, caregiver, deliveryman, street vendor, porter, housecleaner, shepherd, fisherman, farm worker, waiter, and entrepreneur. These jobs are overwhelmingly temporary, dead-end, degrading, low-paying, and arduous if not hazardous. Over the past three decades foreigners have assumed most of the worst jobs on the island and Sicilians have come to depend on them even as they reject the dirty work ever more closely associated with this marginalized population. This book addresses the lives and work of immigrant men and women pursuing three forms of dirty work. In the next chapter we establish the context of immigration to southern Europe generally and to Sicily in particular, and describe the methods and aims of the study. In chapter 3 we examine the women and men of diverse origins who care for Sicilian homes and their occupants in Palermo. The North African men who toil in the greenhouses of southeast Sicily are the subject of chapter 4. In chapter 5 we return to Palermo to examine the plight of Nigerian women, trafficked by co-national criminal gangs, who sell sex on the streets of the city. In conclusion, we consider the future prospects for immigrants in Sicily and the Italian north, and relate the twin processes of immigration and dirty work in Sicily to the wider world.

The three case studies illustrate prominent themes in the newcomer experience. Given the growing demand for elder care and increasing numbers of Sicilian women in the workforce, foreign women and men in urban Sicily have readily found employment caring for Sicilians and their dwellings. In the countryside, nearly all male foreigners have toiled in the island's innumerable vineyards, orchards, and pastures, or aboard fishing fleets. Immigrant women predominate in street prostitution, the most visible and dangerous segment of a growing commercial sex industry. Although street prostitution involves far fewer individuals than the other two fields of endeavor, it touches on widespread concerns over trafficking and immigrant criminality. Offering cheap care, food, and sex, immigrants underwrite lifestyles that Sicilians have come to take for granted even as they worry that the immigrant presence will change life on the island.

Conceptual considerations have also guided our analysis. Scholars have shown that employment is one of the most important determinants of the immigrant situation.[2] According to the influential model developed by sociologists Alejandro Portes and Rubén Rumbaut, the actual economic performance of immigrants is strongly conditioned by government policy and practice, the labor market, and the character of co-ethnic communities. Of course, job prospects and economic security are linked to the work experience, skills, and capital of individuals and families. But, all things being equal, immigrants are more likely to succeed to the extent that they have legal status, possess cultural and physical traits similar to the majority population, and enjoy contact with successful and well-connected co-ethnics. Faring much worse are those populations who lack legal status, possess cultural and physical traits distinct from the host population, and habitually interact with co-nationals lacking in resources. These "contexts of reception" are intertwined; precarious legal status, a meager network or one composed of only working-class folk, and darker skin color all channel individuals into the lower tiers of the labor market. While Portes and Rumbaut developed this model to explore the variable incorporation of newcomers in the United States, the model aptly captures the main lines of the immigrant experience in Sicily, including the three sectors at issue in this study.[3]

Anthropologists and sociologists often center analysis of immigration on nationalities or ethnic groups. This analytical strategy has told us much about cultural encounters, networks, and transnational ties linking immigrants and home communities. While recognizing the striking diversity of immigrant origins in Sicily, we have chosen to orient analysis around sectors.[4] A focus on the participation of newcomers in specific occupations, rather than on ethnic groups per se, generates a different perspective.[5] Attention to fields of endeavor, each with its own particular dynamic and history, situates immigrant labor within specific legal, cultural, and social fields. A sector-based approach also reveals the salience of network and ethnic and racial stereotypes and makes plain the nature of interactions between immigrants and employers. Finally, this perspective directs attention to the profound consequences of immigrant labor for the native born and to their dependency on others from afar.

Dirty Work also departs from the common focus on a single location. We describe experiences of foreigners of diverse origins in rural as well as urban areas of Sicily. Geographically, the analysis centers on Palermo, Sicily's largest city and regional capital, and on the province Ragusa to the island's southeast; it also draws on research in the far Italian north among immigrants formerly resident in Palermo. The inclusion of multiple research sites points to the variety of distinct places in which newcomers make their way and captures, in ways a traditional single-site ethnography could not, the mobility so characteristic of immigrants today.

Domestic service, sex work, and agricultural labor exemplify the dead-end, poorly paid, and risky jobs performed by foreign workers in Sicily and far beyond. Contemporary capitalism creates a demand for what is euphemistically known as "flexible" labor inputs. In practice, this means that in the context of an increasingly competitive, global marketplace, many employers seek to lower the costs of business by hiring temporary and non-unionized workers. Recent immigrants, many of whom are disadvantaged by nationality and race, legal status, and lack of linguistic and other skills, disproportionately accept such employment. Media images and networks of family and friends abroad cultivate the aspiration to leave home while a burgeoning migration industry (represented by a host of legitimate and informal organizations) stands ready to facilitate this movement. The ability of receiving (and sending) governments to manage these flows, while a matter of lively debate and keen interest among policy makers and scholars, is clearly far from adequate. The Sicilian case illustrates the pervasiveness of dirty work in the world economy and points to the unexpected, even intimate, interactions between immigrants, their families, and host populations.

NOTES

1. The Population Division of the Department of Economic and Social Affairs of the United Nations (2006) counted 190,633,564 international migrants as of 2005, up from 176,735,772 in 2000.

2. An incomplete list would include: Castles and Kosack 1985; Castles and Miller 1998; Dale and Cole 1999; Lamphere 1992; Lamphere, Stepick, and Grenier 1994; and Wolf 1982; on southern Europe, see the references in note 1, chapter 2.

3. Portes and Rumbaut have developed their influential model in a series of publications (e.g., Portes and Rumbaut 1996, 2001a, 2001b). Schmitter-Heisler (1998) found that applying the model to the German situation pointed to important similarities and differences in the constraints and opportunities faced by immigrants in the two societies.

4. Anthropologists, like their colleagues in allied disciplines, have long studied migration and economic endeavors (or more generally, work), but they have rarely focused on migrants at work in specific sectors. Exceptions include studies of factory workers (e.g., Lamphere 1987), farm workers (e.g., Wells 1996), and domestics (e.g., Hondagneu-Sotelo 2001). Ortiz (2002) reviews anthropological contributions to labor markets and control and calls for increased attention to the role of migration.

5. A sector-based analysis also permits comparison. In different ways, Brettell and Hollifield (2000), Portes and Rumbaut (1996), and Lucassen and Lucassen (1997) all make convincing arguments for paying greater attention to comparison (across time, space, immigrant populations, and destination countries for example) in migration studies.

2

~~~

The World Comes to Sicily

Before we delve into the lives of immigrant maids and prostitutes in Palermo and agricultural workers in southeastern Sicily, it behooves us to consider the broader political and economic contexts in which their lives unfold. In turn, we examine changing immigrant employment in contemporary southern Europe, Italy's transformation to an immigrant destination, and the contours of the newcomer experience in Sicily. Because anthropological projects are as much the product of human interactions and experiences as theoretical concerns, we close the chapter with a description of the methods and aims of our research.

THE NEW SOUTHERN EUROPE

Sicily's newfound dependence on immigrants exemplifies a distinctive regional pattern. Italy, Portugal, Spain, Greece, Cyprus, and Turkey share a number of features that have a bearing on the reception and incorporation of foreign domestic workers.[1] Southern Europe is characterized by weak welfare states, a graying demographic profile, high rates of official unemployment, a flourishing informal sector, and dynamic small- and medium-sized businesses. The countries of this region were long characterized by massive emigration and have only recently become immigrant destinations in their own right. Notwithstanding national differences, labor demand and government practice and policy across the region have combined to channel the majority of newcomers into unregulated, untaxed, and undocumented jobs—the so-called informal economy.

9

From the late 1980s well into the 1990s, mass entries combined with few avenues for legalization produced a semi-legal population of foreigners vulnerable to exploitation in the workplace. Tolerated by regulatory agencies accustomed to prevalent informal arrangements between employers and employees, the newcomers nevertheless risked legal troubles and deportation. Renting or squatting in decrepit apartments, congregating in the seediest urban areas, and visible in their roles as consumers and workers, immigrants came to be seen as harbingers of disorder and living proof of the incompetence and hypocrisy of southern European governments.

Large numbers of newcomers have accepted dirty work while natives, buoyed by state and family supports, shun such work as unworthy.[2] From Spain to Greece immigrant men tend to find work in fields, orchards, services, and construction; an exception to this rule is the demand for factory workers in northern Italy. In a region where families traditionally carry responsibility for the care of children and the elderly and where states cannot or will not provide sufficient services, immigrant women readily find employment caring for homes and their inhabitants. Exploiting porous borders and human misery and addiction, entrepreneurs and criminal organizations—foreign and homegrown—have developed illicit markets in arms, contraband, and people. In this context, the sizable influx of foreign women has contributed to the recent proliferation in prostitution, club entertainment, and other forms of commercial sex. In the usage of scholars, immigrants participate in labor markets that are "gendered," as occupations tend to be sex-specific; they are also "segmented" or unevenly distributed over space and populations and characterized by disparities in pay, security, and prestige. Thus in Sicily we will find Filipina women clustered in domestic work, Nigerian women in street prostitution, and North African men in fields and greenhouses.

Contemporary immigration provides a telling contrast to the massive post World War II movement, which saw millions of Spaniards, Portuguese, Maltese, Turks, and of course Italians assume the dirty work across the Alps and the Pyrenees. Like the southerners in the north in the postwar period, today's new immigrants to the south confront negative stereotypes, endure exploitation and privation, and send money home even as their labor lends a competitive advantage to their new employers. In other respects the earlier movement of labor from southern to northern Europe differs sharply from contemporary patterns. In the past, especially in the initial phases of labor migration, males predominated whereas today women make up almost half of all foreigners resident in the European Union.[3] The lives of immigrants today are characterized by much greater legal and economic instability than were those of their southern European predecessors who toiled in Switzerland, Germany, and France.[4] In the former period, government and industry actively sought out workers from a

limited number of countries, including former colonies and states border-
ing the Mediterranean. These men (and women) typically found employment in factories and construction and settled in the urban heartlands of
booming economies. Male and female immigrants today, by contrast,
come from a great many countries. They are geographically dispersed, residing in countryside and city, in rich and poor areas alike. Unsolicited in
any formal sense, often unauthorized, these newcomers for the most part
lack institutional recognition and support. Thus, they are commonly portrayed as threats to social stability while they are quietly tolerated as
needed labor in all sectors. While traditional racial categories and the prejudices associated with them are no longer legitimate in post-Holocaust
Europe, populations of foreign origin are nevertheless seen as different,
even destabilizing, in a pattern scholars have called the "new" or "cultural" racism.[5] As non-Christian, non-Western, dark-skinned, or some
combination thereof, newcomers and their children routinely confront
discrimination and rejection based on their appearance, creed, and pre-
sumed cultural defects. In contrast, the large numbers of northern European retirees and second-home owners who have altered the economic
dynamic and social tenor of whole southern districts are viewed as a fact
of modern life rather than a disturbing influx of foreigners.[6]

The nature of employment has changed as well. The regular, often
unionized, employment in large construction and industrial concerns that
promoted the integration of southern Europeans in the postwar period of
"Fordist" industrial production has given way to temporary, usually non-
union, work in smaller firms in city and countryside. As Enrico Pugliese
has pointed out, the basic irrelevance of horizontal institutions such as
unions to most contemporary immigrants stymies integration into the
mainstream of host societies. Faced with feeble institutional support,
newcomers turn for jobs, housing, and aid to current and former employers, church and other volunteer programs, and co-nationals. Ethnicity,
then, should be viewed as an adaptive response to the receiving society
and economy rather than an inevitable predilection to associate with
one's own kind.[7]

We do not foresee a reduction in the need for immigrant workers in the
future. In fact, we anticipate that newcomers will continue to play important roles in the three sectors reviewed in this book (as well as others associated with a more permanent immigrant population). Given longer life
expectancy, birth rates far below replacement rates, diminishing state
services, and a shortage of old-age facilities, European families will turn
increasingly to immigrant caregivers. Mediterranean farmers today face
extremely difficult challenges, and the imminent expansion of the European Union (EU) promises only increased competition and reduced supports. Turning to cheaper foreign workers remains one of the few avenues

for cost cutting available to farmers. The future of foreign sex workers is harder to predict. The adoption of EU-wide measures to combat trafficking and international criminality, together with stepped-up police action and cooperation, may well reduce the numbers of foreign sex workers and deflect the trade elsewhere. Such efforts may simply drive foreign prostitutes off the streets and town squares and into apartments and brothels. Or they may spur traffickers to develop novel and more effective strategies for the infiltration of southern European markets. In any event, the growing and demonstrable appetite for sex for sale among Europeans suggests that the market, however configured, will continue to thrive.

IMMIGRANT ITALY

Italy, always a meeting place for people, ideas, and goods, is more diverse today than ever before. This profound and ongoing transformation dates to the 1970s, a decade in which the massive postwar emigration of Italians slackened and small numbers of foreigners began to settle. Immigration picked up sharply toward the end of the 1980s, surged in the early 1990s, and increased again at the century's close.[8] The number of foreigners holding a "permit to stay" (*permesso di soggiorno*) rose from 355,431 in 1982 to 1,251,994 in 1999, and again to 1,512,324 in 2002.[9] Initially clustered in Rome and the south, today most foreigners are found in the Eternal City and in urban areas of the center-north of Italy. Newcomers have been attracted to Italy by many factors. These include ease of entry relative to traditional destinations such as France and Germany, employment opportunities, lax internal control, social safety nets offered by church and secular organizations, the possibility of regularization through amnesties and legislation (in 1986, 1990, 1995, 1998, and 2002), and, in the case of North Africans and Eastern Europeans, proximity.

People settle in Italy for many reasons. Western Europeans and North Americans do business in Italy or choose to retire there. As the institutional center of the Catholic world, the country draws thousands of religious personnel annually. Military personnel and their families, especially U.S. citizens, cluster around Italy's NATO bases. Others seek refuge from conflicts near and far. But most immigrants come for work or to join family members who are employed.[10] While newcomers usually hail from poorer countries, many come from urban areas and middle-class backgrounds. Long concentrated in services and agriculture, increasing numbers find employment in manufacturing, particularly in the center-north. In all sectors native-born and foreign workers rarely compete directly because the latter perform the most undesirable tasks. Even with high rates of unemployment, particularly in the south and among youth, Italians avoid such dirty work. Buoyed by family and state supports, animated by status aspirations born of educational attainment and high consumption standards, and wary of entering the bottom reaches of a rigid labor market, most Italians refuse to act as servants or toil in fields. Newcomers, often obligated to pay debts incurred in travel and to support families at home, are in no position to refuse such work. As certain jobs become associated with a downtrodden population of foreigners, they become even less palatable to Italian youth and their parents. The declining number of Sicilian youths entering agriculture and domestic service illustrates this dynamic.

Despite their small (but steadily growing) numbers relative to foreign populations elsewhere in Europe and North America,[11] immigrants in Italy render an indispensable service to the Italian economy. As a workforce predisposed to perform arduous and degrading tasks for meager compensation and compelled to accept undocumented employment or short-term contracts, immigrants contribute to the continued viability of countless enterprises and permit higher consumption standards among Italians. The manner in which immigrants make this contribution varies according to the character of local labor markets, of which there are four basic types according to sociologist Maurizio Ambrosini.[12] In the first type of labor market, characteristic of the so-called third Italy of the northeast and parts of Lombardy, small and medium-sized industrial firms seek foreign men for stable and documented if arduous employment. The second type is found in large urban centers, where families and employers in services and construction seek foreign men or women for low-level positions such as caretakers and common laborers, often employing them off the books. Throughout the rural south, immigrants cluster in seasonal, typically undocumented employment in agriculture and sometimes in tourism. Yet a fourth pattern prevails in the rural center-north, where immigrants assume seasonal, increasingly documented, jobs in tourism and agriculture. Ambrosini's typology reminds us that while employers may think of them principally in terms of cheap labor, immigrants are not an undifferentiated mass. Rather, newcomer participation in Italian society is strongly conditioned by the configuration of local labor markets. As we will see, Sicilian urban and rural labor markets, representing the second and third types, offer ample possibilities for employment even—or especially—to those without permits, with consequences for the integration and mobility of newcomers.

Participation in any labor market takes place within institutional and political contexts. In an effort to avoid paying the substantial sums involved in taxes and mandatory contributions to health and pension systems, some employers and employees agree on informal (and illegal) arrangements. Desiring flexibility and obligated to send remittances and repay loans, and perhaps lacking the leverage of legal status, many foreigners accept undocumented employment, commonly referred to as "black work." Recourse to such informality entails serious problems for the majority of foreigners whose permits are linked to documented employment. Immigrants did not create the informal sector, of course, but they have made significant contributions to it, thanks to the tacit approval of police, labor inspectors, and other government officials. Weak internal controls on immigrant employment point to the quiet recognition by the state of the importance of the informal economy. Comments Giuseppe Sciortino: "The existence of a significant population of undocumented immigrants and of many amnesty programs may . . . be viewed as consequences not of failing immigration control but rather of the special, well-entrenched mode of relationship between the Italian state and Italian society."[13] In other words, the arrival of immigrants did not so much transform Italian labor markets as provide a new and more vulnerable workforce for pre-existing and prevalent informal arrangements.

While most Italian politicians agree that foreign workers provide an economic benefit to the country, immigration itself remains a hotly contested issue. At least since the "Albanian crisis"—which saw the initial welcome of tens of thousands refugees from the former Communist dictatorship turn into a messy, mass repatriation all within the span of a few months in 1991—immigration has symbolized disorder, a worrisome sign that the state is incapable of maintaining control over its own borders.[14] Continued illegal entries, particularly along the coasts of Sicily (including its islands, such as Lampedusa) and Puglia, regularly garner intensive media coverage as a "clandestine emergency."[15] European Union member states to the north have called for stricter controls in Italy, asserting that Italy's frequent amnesties beckon aspiring immigrants who will eventually cross the Alps to join their own sizable immigrant populations. Widespread undocumented residence and employment of foreigners within Italy's borders can be portrayed as both symptom and cause of social and political decline. Given high levels of formal unemployment, the political pressure on Italy exerted by EU neighbors, the logistical challenges of monitoring thousands of miles of coastline, and media attention on unauthorized boat arrivals, no politician can afford to appear less than tough on limiting and controlling illegal immigration. As a result, Italian government officials often adopt tough public stances on border surveillance and workplace controls that are contradicted by the realities of daily border crossings, large-scale unauthorized residence, and acknowledged dependency on a foreign workforce.

Map 2.1.　Map of Italy

IMMIGRATION TO SICILY

In a country well known for massive emigration, Sicily has lost prodigious numbers of its sons and daughters. In the late nineteenth and early twentieth centuries, hundreds of thousands of peasants sought refuge from repression and poverty in faraway South and North America. The exodus of the postwar period, in contrast, saw most settle in the heavy industrial districts of the Italian northwest or journey across the Alps to Switzerland, Germany, and France. Sicilian emigrants toiled

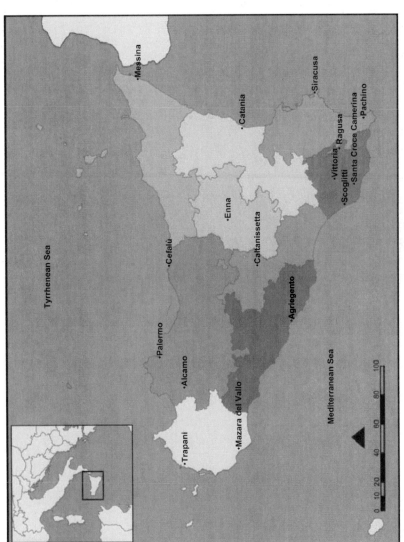

Map 2.2.   Map of Sicily

in services, construction, and industry, providing essential labor for Western Europe's postwar boom. Almost half a million Sicilians left home in the decade 1950–1960 alone. As the departures of emigrants slackened in the early 1970s, immigrants from African, Asia, and elsewhere began to arrive.[16]

In Palermo and Catania, the island's largest metropolitan centers, foreign women arrived to serve the rich who no longer found sufficient numbers of local women willing to clean house and care for the elderly and children. Catholic missionaries from Italy stationed in Mauritius, Cape Verde, and the Philippines organized this influx, at least initially. At about the same time, agriculturalists in Trapani province turned to Tunisian men as the 1968 earthquake in the Belice Valley exacerbated the shortage of field workers.[17] Fleet owners in Mazara del Vallo made particularly aggressive use of the undocumented foreigners in a successful effort to cut costs and weaken fishermen's unions. While the seasonal nature of labor demands in the countryside drew a temporary Tunisian presence, the lengthy fishing season created a permanent and sizable Tunisian enclave in the ancient port city.

The numbers of these early arrivals grew in chain fashion over the following decade. By the mid-1980s the Tunisian presence had spread from Trapani province to the fields, pastures, and quarries along the southern coast of Sicily. Toward the end of the decade, immigration flows swelled and diversified, bringing among others Moroccans, Senegalese, Ghanaians, Ivorians, and Sri Lankans. Entries continued to increase through much of the 1990s, including sizable new flows from Albania, Bangladesh, Romania, and China. These numbers declined somewhat with the new century. In numerical terms, foreigners holding permits to stay numbered 18,888 (1985), 61,523 (1990), 68,854 (1996), 56,736 (1999), 47,904 (2001), and 49,579 (2002).[18]

These figures should be treated with caution for several reasons. Unauthorized aliens do not appear in the count, many foreigners registered in Sicily actually reside elsewhere (usually in the north), minors often lack their own permits, and counting of duplicate and cancelled permits bedeviled the tallies, at least in the 1990s. While the exact number of foreigners is unknown, official numbers do reflect important trends. Immigration to Sicily has surged before and during regularization programs and declined after foreigners received permits and moved on.

It is significant that, despite high unemployment and an anemic economy, Sicily boasted the second largest concentration of foreigners for any region south of Rome in 2001.[19] Over two-thirds of foreigners were concentrated in the provinces of Palermo (13,170), Catania (11,437), and

Messina (7,987), all of which are dominated by eponymous cities. There were also significant numbers of immigrants in provinces dedicated to intensive agriculture, notably Ragusa (5,844), Agrigento (2605), Trapani (2601), and Siracusa (2467), and many fewer in the interior provinces of Caltanisetta (1,182) and Enna (605). In the same year, permit holders from Tunisia, Sri Lanka, Morocco, the United States, Mauritius, Albania, and the Philippines headed the list.[20] In all but the interior provinces, then, foreign faces constitute a visible presence in Sicily today. Their uneven geographical distribution reflects their different patterns of incorporation in local labor markets. Most Tunisians, Moroccans, and Albanians reside in rural areas where they work in agriculture while Sri Lankans, Mauritians, Filipinos, and Bangladeshis cluster in large cities where the service sector is dominate. Likewise, women from Nigeria but also South America, Albania, and states of the former Soviet Union cluster in cities where the commercial sex industry is found.

In the case of Palermo, immigrants reside throughout the city, with notable concentrations in the decrepit historic center and in working-class neighborhoods such as Borgo Vecchio and Zisa. On weekends, immigrant families gather in parks, perhaps treating their children to a carnival ride in the Giardino Inglese, one of the city's better parks. In some neighborhoods, foreign faces predominate in child-care facilities and elementary schools. Mosques, temples, and masses and services in English and other languages bespeak a new religious diversity. From the late 1990s, dozens of immigrant-run shops have sprung up, catering to Sicilians and co-nationals. Along the Via Maqueda, a principal street in the old city, the foreigner can send money home, place international calls, and purchase calling cards from any one of the ubiquitous "phone centers." Also for sale are myriad items, including wooden carvings from West Africa, Tunisian ceramics and fabrics, spices and frozen fish from Bangladesh, and *halal* meat prepared in compliance with the tenets of Islam. At night, discos feature Cape Verdean disk jockeys while young Nigerian women sell sex along major thoroughfares and in parks.

As is true of the region as a whole, Palermo's foreign population has risen and fallen in line with amnesty programs and local economic conditions; it has also grown with continuing family reunification. The mix of peoples has changed too. Thousands of early arrivals from the Ivory Coast and Ghana left in the late 1990s, most for the industrial districts of the north. Bangladeshis and Moroccans arrived in the same period, and Sri Lankans continued to select Palermo as a destination point. As of early 2003, city officials estimated 5,000–7,000 unregistered

Photo 2.1. Immigrant video shop, Palermo

foreigners and counted 16,593 registered foreigners, up from 15,288 in 2000. Sri Lankans, Tunisians, Bangladeshis, Mauritians, Moroccans, and Filipinos headed the list.[21] The figures represent an almost 50 percent increase over the 10,949 registered foreigners tallied for 1998. Because the immigrant population islandwide was very large in 1998, the most recent figures for Palermo may indicate a new surge in the numbers of foreigners resident in Sicily.

The foreign population in Sicily is nothing if not diverse. Newcomers hail from dozens of countries, some a mere ferry trip away, others on the far side of the planet, some peaceful, others torn by civil strife. Immigrants profess most major faiths and a few obscure ones. Adults of working age predominate, but there are growing numbers of children and young adults. Some newcomers quickly master Italian while others struggle with the language for decades. They are urbanites and country folk, professionals and peasants. Most join kith or kin, but some brave it alone. Some relish the freedom, mobility, and access to consumer goods in Italy while others hanker after the familiar smells, tastes, and customs of home. Any immigrant's legal status and employment can, and often does, change, with profound results, as in the case of Augustine described in the previous chapter.

Photo 2.2.   Immigrant festival, Villa Lampedusa, Palermo

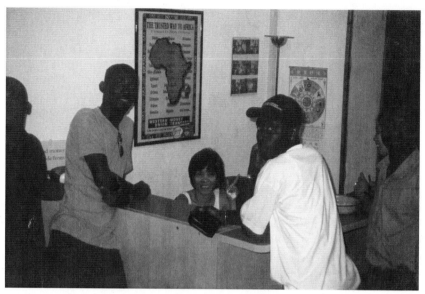

Photo 2.3.   Farah Maija and customers, phone center, Palermo

Photo 2.4.   Street scene, Palermo

UNSETTLING INTEGRATION

Amid this diversity common features stand out. While the following observations are distilled from our experiences in the city of Palermo and
the provinces of Trapani and Ragusa, we believe they speak to the immigrant situation across the island. With the exception of children joining
families, foreigners arrive in search of employment and that quest defines
their existence, at least in the initial years. The Sicilian labor market is
characterized by the prevalence of small firms, high rates of official unemployment, especially among youth, and much informality. With little
industry, few large employers, and weak unions, most Sicilians lack access to the stabilizing force of such horizontal institutions that are prevalent in the Italian north. Secure, well-paying jobs do exist, but these rare
prizes go to those with the winning combination of credentials, expertise,
and the sponsorship of important persons. Clientelism, or the competition
for and distribution of rewards along fluid, personalistic chains of patrons
and clients, represents an important way Sicilians attempt to secure political or economic advantage. Despite recent reforms, such as the ongoing
antimafia movement, most Sicilians think it prudent to cultivate instru-
mental friendships.[22]

Foreigners, typically lacking the influential "recommendation" of well-
placed individuals, the required Italian educational degrees, and perhaps
even a valid permit, are shunted to dirty work as caregivers, cleaners,
dishwashers, fishermen, shepherds, and agricultural day laborers. Others
go into business, hawking sunglasses and jewelry on the streets or
beaches, selling goods at weekly markets in the provinces, or opening
their own storefronts. While such endeavors might promise autonomy,
they can involve pay-offs to local and co-national criminal groups who
control streets and wholesale operations.[23] In either case, immigrants are
forced to rely on their own networks with co-nationals and employers for
jobs, housing, and information. It is no coincidence that virtually all immigrant associations in Palermo bring together people sharing a national
or regional identity. With time, the immigrant may be able to improve her
living situation, perhaps securing an apartment with hot water and a full
bathroom. And by performing satisfactorily on the job, she may receive
more hours or a better job through employers past and present or through
friends of employers. There are, however, very definite limits placed on
an immigrant's ability to pursue a career and gain a purchase on a stable
future.

Immigrants, especially those who have made steps up the occupational
ladder, invariably express frustration with what they describe as the duplicity they encounter among Sicilians. They say that Sicilians are hard on
each other and acknowledge the marked class divisions of Sicilian society

and its brutal expressions in the workplace and on the streets. But there comes a time in every interview or at every dinner when the immigrant gives vent to frustration. Sicilians, they assert, often extend a helping hand to a poor immigrant they deem pitiable, but become uncomfortable when the foreigner succeeds and poses a competitive threat. This fear takes many forms. On important exams, foreigners achieve curiously low marks while their undistinguished Sicilian peers record mysteriously high ones. Paperwork for job applications goes missing, or foreign credentials are subject to review yet another time. Rare lapses in Italian are corrected by people who themselves routinely introduce Sicilian dialect terms into their conversations. Immigrant contributions are minimized, their potential ignored. Foreigners in positions of authority find their competence questioned at every turn, as the following stories reveal.

William, a Sri Lankan longtime resident in Palermo and fluent in Italian, manages an elegant restaurant in an affluent part of the city. When a new deliveryman appeared and asked for the boss, instead of approaching William, the dark-skinned foreigner, as directed by employees, he made a show of directing himself to the Sicilian staff, including the lowly dishwasher. Once he conceded that the foreigner was indeed in charge, he deposited the delivery on the sidewalk rather than in the storeroom as is customary. When William threatened to call the boss of the deliveryman, he grudgingly consented to move the goods inside. As William observed, he could have asked his staff to move the boxes, but at stake was respect rather than mere inconvenience.

Or take James, from Nigeria and Sierra Leone, who serves as a trainer and assistant coach for a professional women's basketball team in a provincial city. Alarmed by the rigidity and cautious attitude of his Italian players, he urges them to become freeflowing, inventive, and aggressive. Their constant lament is, "Don't teach us African basketball," as if that were an acknowledged, inferior approach to the game. Each time, he patiently explains that basketball is American, not African, in origin, and that he learned from Americans and is trying to teach them how the game should be played.

It is significant that both William and James are outgoing, affable men who socialize almost exclusively with Italians. Both routinely confront experiences like the ones described, experiences that for them reveal an attitude too common among Sicilians that immigrants will never measure up to Sicilians. As the players' words suggest, the confidence in the superiority of things Italian or Western draws on enduring racist views of the inherent limitations of non-whites. But it also taps perceptions of the wealth and character of nations, which can be linked to physical appearance in complicated ways. Augustine, for one, distinguished the polite treatment his sister, a U.S. resident, received from Sicilians when she visits with the rudeness with which he is so often greeted. "It's as though, once they know you're from a poor country, they feel it's fine to disrespect you." He has coped with these slights in many ways. He has stayed proud, performed his jobs to the best of his abilities, and made the decision to move north to secure the dignity of stable employment. Midway through the interview described in the first chapter he pulled out two beautiful dress shirts, explaining that after he had received his permit and finally was able to save some money, he had made the purchase at Christmastime. He admitted that he had spent a lot of money on those shirts but stressed that, to have self-respect and enjoy the respect of others, sometimes "you need to be clean and handsome."

The Italian government, while acknowledging the contribution of foreigners to the economy, has been slow to provide needed services. With few exceptions, local governments in Sicily, whether regional, provincial, or municipal, have failed miserably to make provisions for, or merely recognize, these new workers, students, and residents. Stepping into the breach, church-sponsored or affiliated programs provide invaluable assistance for many immigrants, especially new arrivals. Church (and lay) programs exist in most cities and even in small towns with immigrant concentrations; their offerings vary considerably, from seasonal operations established at harvest time to complex, year-round establishments. The largest, such as the Santa Chiara and Caritas centers in Palermo or Caritas offices in the southeastern city of Vittoria (Ragusa province), have at various points offered temporary lodging, meals, medical care, employment information, showers, legal advice, a postal address, a gathering place, and identification cards (in place of passports and other documents that can be held in a safe on the premises).

Immigrants who have participated in the various attempts by the government to grant some kind of voice or role in local affairs to newcomers have become disillusioned both with factionalism among immigrants and inconsistency on the part of Sicilian institutions. Given the prevalence of clientelism and the political insignificance of immigrants (very few have the right to vote), initiatives sponsored by local government have been typically scattershot, uncoordinated, and subject to ulterior personal and political goals.[24] Individuals sadly recall the problems of engaging in immigration initiatives sponsored by local government, including chronic budget shortfalls, delays in pay, and political maneuvering. A Sicilian activist, long involved in immigration issues told us of an intercultural education training program he created for teachers to help them understand and educate immigrant students. In a 2001 interview, he described with bitterness how a local politician took over and mismanaged the program, eventually running it into the ground. Fondly he recalled the heady days of the early 1990s when he dared imagine that a new Palermo could be built together with immigrants. Instead, he lamented, "everything of value has been lost, it's scorched earth now, the same old story." Like many other activists we met, he has withdrawn from volunteer activity.

All immigrants can recount episodes of personal mistreatment, stories revealing what they experience as categorical injustices. Despite these obstacles, many foreigners grow fond of Sicily. Not a few West Africans, noting the pleasant climate, expressive populace, material affluence, and vibrant public life, describe it as a "well-developed African country." Implicit in this observation is the contrasting stereotype, voiced by Augustine, of the Italian north as cold and efficient. Immigrants tend to socialize with other foreigners, but some develop lasting ties and romances, with Sicilians. Many point with pride to the economic contribution of immigrants to the city as a whole, and emphasize their many roles—as residents, consumers, and shop owners—in reviving the old city center. "I have never said, 'Palermo, city of shit,' as so many others do," said a woman from the Philippines in 2003. She acknowledged the infamous corruption and inefficiency of the capital, but regarded the all-too-common phrase as an admission of hopelessness and a dishonorable shirking of responsibility. Through associational activity and volunteer work on behalf of newcomers, she had made her stand and was proud of it.

On balance, the immigrant's life is a precarious, unsettled one. Work can evaporate during a downturn in the local economy, and even in good times getting paid in full can be a challenge in a society in which a glut of workers and prevalence of informal arrangements afford palpable power to employers. All agree that foreigners pay exorbitant rates for housing, much in very poor repair. According to newcomers, poor and ignorant Sicilians blatantly express their prejudices while the affluent remain convinced of the superiority of Western culture even as they mouth the rhetoric of multiculturalism. Newcomers confront forms of abuse as well. Sicilian men, regarding foreign women as sexually available, openly proposition them. In poor neighborhoods of Palermo in the early 1990s, residents would throw food at immigrants or prod their children to hurl abuse of one form or another. Immigrants also complain of the unwanted attentions of local thieves. As a rule, immigrants tend to be cautious and self-effacing lest they provoke a Sicilian tough or become entangled in a bureaucratic snare. While the police concentrate their energies on troublemakers and tolerate law-abiding foreigners regardless of legal status, immigrants, especially those lacking papers, give the police a wide berth and avoid government offices. Under these strains, far from home, some submit to loneliness, falling into a funk or reaching for the bottle. Others buoy themselves with calls, or more rarely trips, home. They enjoy spending time with friends and attending frequent events staged by cultural or religious organizations or by an ever-changing roster of immigrant associations, the posters for which decorate many old city walls.

Given the fundamental insecurity of immigrant life in Sicily, many leave for the north or other countries. Some do make a home in Sicily. Perhaps their spouse is Sicilian, perhaps their family has settled in, or they are put off by the burden of a prospective move and much higher cost of living in the north. Perhaps they have experienced the minor miracle of obtaining stable, clean, documented employment in Sicily. A select few act as intermediaries between new arrivals and prospective employers or Sicilian institutions and politicians. In this way they can render public service, assist those in need, and gain personal advantage, not necessarily in that order.

But many have left or are busy contemplating a move north, typically for financial considerations. "You know that one wage here supports twenty or thirty people back home. We have heavy obligations to earn money," remarked a man who had moved from Palermo to an industrial center close to the Swiss border in order to fulfill his duty to his family in the Ivory Coast. Paradoxically, gaining legal status can also compel an immigrant northward. To retain legal status, an immigrant (head of household) must demonstrate employment, a legal procedure many Sicilian employers would prefer to avoid. Some, particularly Sri Lankans, leave the country altogether, bound for the large diasporas in Canada or England. Populations specializing in domestic work (Cape Verdeans, Mauritians, and Filipinos above all) have sought superior pay and working conditions in Rome, Milan, and other center-north cities. Others cluster in the industrial districts of the north that have experienced severe labor shortages for much of the last decade. While the news media and employment agencies act as occasional signposts, the path northward is paved with personal connections. Immigrants call or visit friends and family installed in the north, and meet them when they return "home" to Palermo for the holidays. Geographic and occupational mobility and the quest for stable and preferably cleaner work are the stuff of countless immigrant stories. In each of the following case studies we will chart newcomer mobility and in the concluding chapter we will consider how the current pattern replicates Sicily's historic role as a provider of labor for northern industry.

THE RESEARCH PROJECT

Our interest in immigration to Sicily dates to the late 1980s. In 1988, in the course of Booth's dissertation research on earthquake reconstruction, we came to appreciate the indispensable role played by Tunisians in the fields and in the fishing fleet of Trapani province. Two years later, Cole's dissertation research on the everyday and political reactions of Sicilians to immigration established links to people and institutions concerned with newcomers. While the present work draws on these prior experiences, it is based primarily on collaborative research conducted periodically from 1998 to 2004.[25] We found that repeat visits—a necessity given our teaching schedules and parenting duties—in fact afforded us an unexpected vantage point onto the dynamism of immigrant life. In this way we came to appreciate the changing fortunes of individuals. We saw clearly the characteristic mobility of newcomers. Our immigrant acquaintances of one summer would receive permits and depart for the north, and we would come to know new arrivals to this island of informal labor markets and flexible attitudes toward questions of legal status.

In the summer of 1998, we set out to discern the main lines of immigrant work and integration in Palermo. On the basis of that research we designed a project aimed at collecting life histories of domestic workers, which we began the following summer. At the same time we became interested in the newcomer experiences in other sectors and locations. In Palermo itself, we sought out immigrant domestics and entrepreneurs as well as people working with Nigerian prostitutes. In excursions to the island's southwest and southeast we observed the mighty contribution of Tunisians to agricultural enterprises. We pursued a similar tact again in 2001. In 2002, intrigued by immigrant mobility, we visited a group of Ivorians formerly resident in Palermo and now laboring in factories north of Milan. By Easter 2003, with the present manuscript taking shape, field research focused on the themes of prostitution in Palermo and greenhouse agriculture in the Vittoria and Santa Croce Camerina area of southeastern Sicily, a line of inquiry that we pursued again the following year. Ultimately we settled on the theme of work because it stands at the center of the immigrant experience. We chose to focus on the three forms of dirty work because they throw into sharp relief some of the most characteristic dilemmas and contributions of immigrant life in Sicily (and beyond). As mentioned earlier, we were guided as well by the conviction that a focus on occupation could reveal patterns and perspectives missed by the more common focus on nationalities and ethnic groups.

We learned much about the many situations of newcomers from discussions and interviews with concerned journalists, scholars, and representatives, both foreign and Italian, of unions, churches, and associations. Interviews with associational personnel afforded insight into educational, cultural, and political efforts to give voice to newcomers. Union spokespersons described local labor markets and the laws that apply, or should apply, to foreign workers. And because they aid immigrants in so many ways, representatives of church centers proved extremely valuable sources. They also possessed unique long-term perspectives on immigrant work and experience and on the changing composition of the foreign populations they encountered.

As ethnographers, we endeavored to immerse ourselves in a variety of immigrant environments. We paid routine visits to important gathering places like Catholic and Protestant centers and select old city neighborhoods. We attended celebrations and meetings sponsored by immigrant and multicultural associations. We spent a lot of time hanging around in businesses offering the telephone and money transfer services so important to foreigners. While immigrants waited for calls and receipts, we discussed ties to home countries, family members' expectations of money and support, and the stresses of life abroad. We visited and, whenever possible, patronized immigrant shops and eateries. Over coffee, ice cream, or a meal we chatted with immigrants about their problems and prospects and what seemed like the inexorable pull of the north. Without fail immigrants quizzed us about the place of newcomers in the United States. We accompanied immigrants on their daily rounds. In makeshift kitchens in the halls of crumbling mansions, we learned to cook dishes from Ghana and the Philippines. We hosted immigrants in our temporary home and over long meals heard stories of family, friends, and life in home countries. And we conducted dozens of interviews—some brief, others in-depth—with foreigners of diverse origins. Some of these encounters were serendipitous while others were facilitated by the efforts of institutional representatives or mutual friends who vouched for our integrity. People, we found, were most comfortable relating their experiences and perspectives in the form of stories. A discussion of eating habits, for example, could serve as an introduction to a story about how work in a Sicilian home or restaurant had honed skills in the kitchen and shaped food preferences. Or, talk about the average working day could lead to bitter reminiscences of experiences of discrimination at work, on the bus, or in the doctor's office.

Our status as a husband-wife team certainly influenced these encounters. As a rule, we interviewed associational and institutional representatives together, taking turns writing notes and posing questions. With immigrants we found that same-sex interviews tended to work best. (For the sake of simplicity, throughout the text we employ the first-person plural pronoun to describe observations and interview encounters.) Our two young children often accompanied us on these and other forays; their presence brought levity to the enterprise, and their questions and interactions with immigrant friends could take conversation in unexpected and interesting directions.

Our status as United States citizens also conditioned our experiences. For some—ardent Leftists and Muslim fundamentalists come to mind—

our nation's policies and leadership inevitably became a topic of discussion and, with the war in Iraq, the first topic of discussion. Yet even in these cases we managed to speak at length about the immigrant experience. Most immigrants welcomed our attentions and participated willingly in the project. It was not uncommon for what was planned as a brief chat to turn into a three- or four-hour session combining elements of a chat, structured interview, and confessional. Many felt comfortable voicing criticisms of Sicilian and Italian society to us because, for them, the United States, whatever its flaws, grants immigrants opportunities unrivaled elsewhere. As foreigners and non-residents, we were not linked to any group or institution and had no stake in the legal status or associational aspirations of those interviewed. And for people who smart from lack of recognition, the prospect of being treated seriously by scholars was profoundly gratifying. As an Ivorian man remarked at the end of one of these marathon discussions, "We carry so much inside all the time; it feels good to let it out."

NOTES

1. For analyses of southern Europe see Anthias and Lazaridis 2000; King and Ribas-Mateos 2002; King 2000; Mingione and Quassoli 2000; Reyneri 2003, 1998; Sciortino 1999; and Solé and Parella 2003.

2. It is true that immigrants are associated with dirty work and disorder across Europe. This tendency is most pronounced in the southern countries, like Italy, where governments were unprepared for the historic novelty of immigration, and where the overwhelming majority of newcomers are or once were illegal and have accepted undocumented employment at the lowest rungs of the economic ladder. In contrast, the much deeper histories of mass immigration in France, the United Kingdom, and Germany have produced a more varied outcome. Immigrants and their children in northern Europe count among their ranks influential entrepreneurs, soccer stars, schoolteachers, police officers, novelists, film directors, sociologists, and more.

3. In 2000, females made up 39.1 percent of foreigners resident in the European Union and 45.8 of foreigners in Italy (Caritas di Roma 2003: 50). Many immigrant populations exhibit gender imbalances. In 2002, females accounted for the following percentages of foreign populations resident in Italy: Moroccans (33.1), Albanians (40.9), Romanians (53.5), Filipinos (64.7), Chinese (47.6), and Tunisians (25.6) (Caritas di Roma 2003: 495). On the gendered nature of immigration, and the increasing numbers of women on the move, see, among others, Andall 2003; Anthias and Lazaridis 2000; and Castles and Miller 1998.

4. This description refers to trends and does not suggest that the early period was totally regulated or a satisfying experience for all. For a general account of the postwar "guest worker" system, see Castles and Kosack 1985. In the case of Portugal, mandatory military service was extended to four years in the mid-1960s

and it was a crime to leave the country without a passport until the 1974 revolution; perhaps two-thirds of all Portuguese immigrants in France 1950–70 arrived illegally (Brettell 2003).

5. Balibar (1991), Cole (1997), and Stolcke (1995), among others, discuss new forms of racism in Europe.

6. On British retirees in the south, see King, Warnes, and Williams 2000.

7. See Pugliese 1993.

8. For this description of immigration to Italy we have drawn on a number of studies, including Ambrosini 2001; Andall and King 1999; Bonifazi 2000; Caritas di Roma 1997, 2000, 2001, 2002, 2003; Grillo and Pratt 2002; Reyneri 2004a, 2004b; Sciortino 1999; and Zincone 2001.

9. Caritas di Roma 2000: 273; Caritas di Roma 2003: 6.

10. As of 2001, overall 59 percent of foreigners held permits for work and 29 percent for family reunification; in the case of Moroccans, the two categories account for all but about 4,000 of the 158,094 permit holders or about 97 percent (Caritas di Roma 2002: 78, 98).

11. As of 1999, foreigners account for 36 percent of the resident population of Luxembourg, 9.2 of Austria, 8.9 of Germany, 8.8 of Belgium, and 5.6 of France compared to 3.1 in Italy (Caritas di Roma 2002: 35).

12. See Ambrosini 2001: 75.

13. Sciortino 1999: 257.

14. Active in promoting this dark vision have been two parties, the post-fascist National Alliance and the Northern League, both of which rose to prominence with the disintegration of the Italian political class in the scandals of the early 1990s.

15. During the summer of 1998, for example, the liberal daily *La Repubblica* used the phrase as a rubric for daily reports of unauthorized boat landings.

16. Figures for emigration from Sicily come from Renda 1989: 122–23. Caritas di Roma (2002); Booth and Cole (1999); Cole (1997, 2003); Cusumano (1976, 2000); and Hannachi (1998) describe immigration to Sicily.

17. Booth (1997, 1999) describes the aftermath of the earthquake.

18. The figures come from Caritas di Roma 1997: 347; 2002: 431; 2003: 127.

19. These figures come from Caritas di Roma 2002: 431. The same year Sicily had the eighth largest foreign population among Italy's twenty regions.

20. These figures come from Caritas di Roma 2002: 432, 458.

21. This was reported in the February 18, 2003, issue of *Giornale di Sicilia*.

22. On clientelism in the city, see Chubb 1982; on the antimafia struggle, see Schneider and Schneider 2003.

23. Sixteen men from Bangladesh were indicted in 2003 for mafia-style criminal activity in Palermo, including demanding protection money from co-national shopkeepers and window washers (*Giornale di Sicilia*, November 27, 2003). Immigrant street vendors and window washers are also said to "rent" space and equipment from Sicilian thugs (Meli 1998).

24. For example, in 1996, the administration of Leoluca Orlando announced an ambitious program under the title, "Many People, One City: Palermo." The pro-

gram was in keeping with the forward-looking and multicultural approach of a mayor best known for his antimafia stance. Yet the search for publicity, the emphasis on cultural events, and ultimately the lack of concrete results were just as characteristic of his administration.

25. We spent about one month in Sicily in summers of 1998, 1999, and 2001. Booth visited northern Italy in the spring of 2000. Cole visited the north of Italy in 2002 and returned to Sicily in 2003, 2004, and 2006.

3

~~~

Family Support

E very day in Palermo, newcomers clean homes, tend gardens, prepare meals, don maids' uniforms, and care for the elderly. Some earn a monthly salary and receive modest benefits while most cobble together a livelihood from an ever-changing series of weekly appointments. Some regard their activity as a career or as an approximation of one during their sojourn in Italy. Many others, particularly the men who have recently entered this traditionally female sector, see it as a refuge until the next amnesty program offers a permit and the possibility of moving to the Italian north in search of stable employment.

Domestic work is an apt place to begin our review of dirty work. Cleaning and attending to the elderly are by far the most frequent jobs performed by immigrants in Palermo.[1] Rarely have we met an immigrant who has not at one time slung a mop, cleaned dishes, or guided a frail old person through the day. Consideration of the domestic sector reveals that over the past thirty years foreigners have come to predominate as young Sicilians shun work as servants and caregivers. For Sicilian employers, immigrants provide status, comfort, and, perhaps most significant, the possibility of honoring obligations to aging parents. For immigrants, domestic employment too often adversely impacts their own family plans and ties; many find the security to form a family only when they leave the island and obtain work in the north. Finally, because the domestic work involves so many nationalities—a short list of the principal participants would include Filipinos, Mauritians, Cape Verdeans, Sri Lankans, Bangladeshis, Ivorians, and Ghanaians—the sector is also a good place to explore ethnic and racial stereotypes and experiences, the role of networks in occupational and geographical mobility, and the variable integration of immigrants.

THE WIDER CONTEXT

The Palermo case is best understood with reference to Italian and southern European patterns. Foreigners clean and care throughout Italy, especially in urban areas and in the populous and wealthy center-north. As of 1999, non–European Union nationals made up about half of the over 200,000 registered domestics and the same percentage of the estimated 800,000 undeclared workers in the sector. According to Caritas di Roma, almost one-sixth of Italians over the age of sixty-five employ non–European Union citizens.[2] The proportion of foreigners engaged in domestic service will undoubtedly continue to rise in the future as young Italians increasingly reject such work as dead-end and degrading.

The growing reliance of Italians on paid domestic labor springs from several sources. Owing to new opportunities and exigencies, more and more women have joined the labor force. Although the rates of female participation in Italy's labor force lag far behind those of northern Europe, the paucity of child care facilities in Italy relative to France, Denmark, Germany, and elsewhere means Italian working women face great pressures.[3] Despite these new demands, most women remain charged with primary responsibility for care of home and family. At the same time, the greater longevity of the elderly coupled with a trend toward smaller families means that fewer adult (female) children must care for their parents for longer periods. The percentage of the Italian population over sixty-five rose from 12 to 18.2 in the years 1975–2000 while the average number of children per woman fell from 2.28 in 1970–1975 to 1.2 in 1995–2000.[4] Given the predilection of southern Europeans generally for household servants—a pattern all but absent among their northern counterparts—rising incomes and consumption standards also fuel the demand. Given the choice, not a few employers prefer foreign over domestic servants, deeming the former more tractable and prestigious than the native-born. Furthermore, in the context of higher educational attainments and job aspirations, Italian youths and their families are loath to accept what they deem a lowly station.

The policies and practices of the Italian state also figure importantly in these developments. As we saw in the previous chapter, a porous border and lax internal controls permitted the entry, residence, and employment of significant numbers of foreigners through the mid-1990s. Given their precarious legal and financial status, many foreigners accepted dirty work, as undocumented household workers, for example. In the last decade, the Italy has enacted special allowances for the entry and regularization of workers in the domestic sector even as it has imposed visas, increased border controls, and instituted quotas for immigrants in general. Finally, insufficient social services, especially with regard to elder care, have placed great strains on Italian families and sharpened demand for paid domestic labor.

The Sicilian (and Italian) case fits squarely within southern European patterns. From Portugal to Cyprus, immigrants have entered a burgeoning domestic sector for these reasons—lack of elder care, increased participation of women working outside the home, and rising consumption standards. And as in Sicily, foreigners elsewhere often care for the elderly. With falling birthrates and greater longevity, families across southern Europe are forced to cope with increasing numbers of dependent elderly. Private facilities are expensive, uncommon, and not well regarded, and southern European states offer very little in the way of services to the elderly and their families. Greek law, for example, places the responsibility on the shoulders of the family; in the early 1990s, in fact, fewer than one in a hundred Greeks over sixty-five resided in institutions. The Italian state promises more but delivers little in the way of social services. Italy possesses the lowest number of nursing home beds per capita in Europe; only six percent of Italians between seventy-five and eighty-five, and 18 percent of those over eighty-five lived in institutions in the late 1980s.[5] It should come as no surprise then that from the late 1980s the Greek and Italian families who could afford it turned to immigrants. In fact, one in six Italians over sixty-five is cared for by a non-EU citizen, as noted earlier. The role of immigrant caregivers is bound to become more significant given the southern European pattern of families, rather than institutions, caring for the elderly.

According to interview data and emerging scholarship,[6] domestic work entails long hours, tedium, low pay, and, frequently, undocumented employment. Housework, already low status because it is linked to women, assumes an even lower status when performed by another for pay. (There is also the stigma of tradition. In the past domestics always came from the ranks of the poor and needy, as we describe later.) Employers may claim the worker "is one of the family," but these verbal assurances merely mask the obvious status and power differential in the language of family equality. On the positive side, domestic work offers new avenues for self-expression and autonomy even as it imposes problems and costs. For immigrant women living abroad, earning money can mean independence from a demanding father or husband, and a woman's power within her family can grow with her monetary contributions. It can also provide opportunities for an active role in friendship groups and associations made up of women. And employment abroad may enable women to fund family reunification, bringing over a spouse and children or, more rarely, returning home themselves.

Perhaps the single most important distinction of domestic employment is between living-in and living-out. Some employers desire constant service or require round-the-clock care of the elderly or infirm. Others can get by with weekly or daily cleaning and cooking help. For immigrants, living with the employer solves the housing question, significantly reduces living expenses, and increases savings and potential remittances. On the other hand, living and working under one roof means forsaking an independent existence, entails very long hours, and increases vulnerability to economic and sexual exploitation. As a career, being a maid is at odds with family formation and caring for another's child can be bittersweet. In the typical scenario, a woman accepts a live-in position upon arrival; with experience and increased contacts, she moves out of her employer's house, takes an apartment, and commutes to work. The move grants autonomy and makes possible family reunification or formation. But this hard-won freedom is counterbalanced by scheduling problems—live-outs tend to have multiple employers, all with changing requirements—and increased costs. Because the workplace remains located in the privacy of another's home, there is always the possibility for abuse, though not to the extent possible in the live-in situation.

THE RECENT HISTORY OF THE SICILIAN FAMILY

A brief review of the past points to key changes and continuities in the Sicilian family, reveals the gendered division of household labor, and suggests why Sicilians today shun domestic employment. By its very nature, domestic service is intimately connected to family life. In Sicily, as in every society, there exists variation in family form and function. As the research of Jane and Peter Schneider[7] has shown, the nuclear family predominates, and links to family of orientation tend to weaken as individuals form their own families. Like southern Italians generally, Sicilians regard enlarged or expanded family ties as desirable. Ideally, this entails residential propinquity if not household extension, sharing of social reproductive and productive tasks, and frequent social interaction. Historically, circumstances have not been favorable to the expansion of family ties in Sicily. Widespread poverty, malnutrition, short life expectancy, and massive emigration have all buffeted Sicilian families and reduced many to nuclear family forms and their fragments. At the same time, a state run by and for the powerful, including political and economic elites and the mafia, has made family the crucial resource for many Sicilians.

Sicilian women assumed near complete responsibility for the domestic sphere. Wives, often with help from daughters, would maintain the house, prepare food, rear children and prepare them for marriage, and, importantly, provide care for the aged. Men, in turn, were defined as family breadwinners; they also defended family reputation in the community and represented the household in relations with town officials, tax collectors, and other outside authorities. A cycle of poverty, child labor, and limited opportunities, however, forced many Sicilian families to compromise their ideals. In the countryside, women produced crafts, gleaned, and took in wash while men accepted humbling tasks and inadequate wages or went without work. Well into the twentieth century Sicilian elites claimed the labor of whole families of the class of landless and land-poor agricultural laborers, called *braccianti*. Men worked the fields, boys tended animals, girls and young women served as domestics, and wives acted as wet nurses, servants, and laundresses.[8] Laboring men from a small town in the western interior "recall with resentment the gentry's expectation that 'we give up our lives as well as our labor' to be *sempre spostata*, always at their disposition."[9]

In this context, domestic service was a shameful if often necessary form of employment. People assumed that elite men and their sons had their way with poor female employees, an assumption all too often corroborated by foundlings left to institutional care. Emigration offered a way out of grinding poverty, and from the late nineteenth century up to the 1960s hundreds of thousands of Sicilian families sent members overseas, across the Alps, and to the Italian north. Significant improvements in the quality of life were registered in decades after World War II, the result of increasing state supports, emigrant remittances, and a rebounding local economy. Experiences with stable employment, especially outside of Sicily, presented new, less brutally exploitative models of employee-employer relations, and by the mid-1960s the "servile relations" binding peasants and other workers to their masters were a thing of the past. For many, it was far preferable for the husband to journey to Germany than for the wife to expose herself and her family to shame by serving as a maid in the home of a local elite family. Throughout the period of transformation, Sicilian families experienced fragmentation, reunification, and idealization. The family constituted the most important resource in the lives of most people, holding out the possibility of social, economic, and residential security.

The city of Palermo experienced rapid growth from the late 1950s, fueled in large measure by public expenditure (the city is the seat of municipal, provincial, and regional governments). Colluding and competing for fat government contracts, graft, real estate speculation, and outright theft of public property, conservative political figures and organized crime families presided over the transformation of the regional capital.[10] Employment opportunities in construction, services, and the public sector afforded the poor new opportunities for consumption and permitted escape from menial occupations. Consequently, most women withdrew completely from the long hours and stigma of the live-in maid's life; if they remained in the sector, it was on a part-time basis. Residing with their own families and "lending a hand" through hourly cleaning work, poor Sicilian women left the shame of live-in work behind them. Other working-class women pursued employment outside of the sector.

As poor women in Sicily (and elsewhere in Italy) were abandoning (full-time) domestic service, national institutions were engaged in an effort to lend dignity and legal protections to the occupation. Jacqueline Andall has told the story of one of the key players in this struggle, ACLI-COLF,[11] founded in 1946. An explicitly Christian endeavor, the organization promoted the sacrificing, maternal role of the domestic servant and called for harmonious employer-employee relations. While retaining the traditional subservience of the servant's interests to those of the family, however, the organization called for the improvement of working conditions and the regularization of the sector. Emblematic of the organization's stance was the new term for servant, *colf*, an abbreviation of the Italian term *collaboratrice familiare* or "family collaborator." (By the late 1990s, *badante*, or caregiver, had replaced the term in general usage.) In the late 1960s and early 1970s, leading elements within the organization began to view the employer-employee relation in class terms and demand that domestic workers receive rights similar to workers in other sectors. Alarmed at this radical turn, a conservative wing broke off and in 1971 founded a rival institution, API-COLF.[12] With the 1969 legislative redefinition of domestic work as regular (as opposed to atypical) employment, the stage was set for the kind of collectively bargained national contract governing working conditions and other matters typical of other sectors. Both ACLI-COLF and API-COLF were present at the signing of the first such agreement, in 1974, and both have continued to exert an influence in subsequent debate and negotiations.[13] As we will see, API-COLF proved particularly important in the struggle of foreign domestics for fair and legal treatment in Palermo.

FOREIGN MAIDS COME TO PALERMO

With the exodus of Sicilian women from domestic work, the rich turned, as they so often had, to the Church, but this time the Church turned abroad. Catholic organizations, particularly the Salesian order, began to recruit women abroad, and soon immigrants were donning maids' uniforms in Palermo.[14] For the city's rich, a foreign servant became a fashion statement, an emblem of distinction. Active recruitment soon ceased and a chain migration pulling female family members, relatives, and friends consolidated the female-led populations from the Philippines, Cape Verde, and Mauritius. In those years, virtually all immigrant women worked as live-in maids, receiving a monthly salary and receiving one and a half days off per week. Otherwise unseen, they became visible on Thursday afternoons when they would gather along the elegant, tree-lined boulevard, Viale della Libertà, or other public places in the city. On Sundays, they could be seen in church. In the case of Catholic Filipinas, they would gather to hear Don Naselli, a high-ranking Salesian, deliver the mass in English at Santa Lucia. On occasion they would go on the trips he organized to points elsewhere in Sicily and beyond. Some residents of Palermo certainly observed the novel phenomenon before them. However, considered (as women) non-threatening, rarely appearing in public places, and interacting for the most part with employers, co-ethnics, and a limited number of Sicilian institutions, these early arrivals remained all but invisible. Similar patterns developed in Rome, Milan, and other Italian cities.[15]

The pioneers of domestic service recall the 1970s and early 1980s as hard times. Together with fifty other Filipinos, Concetta arrived in 1979. Working in the spacious homes of the city's elite, she learned the arcane customs of that milieu, from elaborate table settings and dinner rituals to correct forms of address for the nobles and professionals who hosted and attended such gatherings. In a 1990 interview, she described how some employers treated the women "like slaves," refusing to pay them or proffering a pittance, threatening to have them deported if they complained to the authorities. Others treated the women with decency, but even they expected round-the-clock service.

In the early 1980s, immigrants and Sicilians fought to secure the rights of domestic workers in the city. Working with a national Filipino organization, Concetta rallied fellow Filipinas. She encouraged them to demand their rights by working only the legal limit of hours per day or, failing that, to engage in a mass walkout. Meanwhile, the Palermo office of API-COLF, itself associated with Don Naselli and the Salesians, provided legal assistance to foreign and domestic workers whose employers were reluctant to honor the national contract. (The contract, which governs pay, working conditions, and benefits, is described later.)

Concetta summarized this "struggle," saying, "We taught employers about our rights, not the other way around." Through such efforts, Filipinos, already prized as dependable and model servants, assumed a dominant place in the pecking order of domestic workers and garnered higher pay and better working conditions. Concetta's pride in the high status enjoyed by Filipinos and her role in gaining it are tempered by resentment:

> I used to have an inferiority complex, but now I realize that I am smarter than most of my employers. They haven't gone anywhere, but I have traveled all over Italy and came round the world from the Philippines. I speak three languages and they know only one, maybe two.

By the late 1980s, foreigners—that is to say, mostly women from the Philippines, Cape Verde, and Mauritius—had come to dominate the live-in market and make inroads into the live-out one. They found work through employers and co-ethnic networks. They could also turn to the busy offices of API-COLF and ACLI-COLF, which, in addition to serving as employment agencies, provided legal assistance, training, and other services to domestic employees.[16]

The effects of moving to live-out work were far-reaching. For some time, the women had persevered as live-ins; living with an employer could be stifling, but it made possible larger remittances and financed housing and education for children back home. Tired of spending their little free time out of doors and desiring a measure of independence, some women began to seek a place of their own. Groups of Filipinas, for example, would rent out an apartment and use it as a kind of social club, gathering there on days to chat, cook, and relax in privacy. With time, numbers of foreign domestics tired of the constraints of the live-in positions and began to move into their own residences. For some, this move was made easier by understanding employers who continued to employ the women as live-outs and by Sicilian friends ready to guide them through Palermo's challenging housing market. In other cases, the transition was traumatic or even stymied as employers demanded that the women stay as a live-in or leave the job altogether and threatened to refuse to act as a reference to prospective employers. By the mid-1980s foreign women had made significant inroads into the live-out market.

THE MARKET EXPANDS

About this time several trends converged to increase and diversify demand for paid domestic labor. Middle-class Sicilian women were increasingly entering the labor market, owning to feminist aspirations, expanded opportunity for higher education and professional employment, and economic necessity.[17] Despite new obligations outside the home, women remain charged with primary responsibility for the maintenance of the home and family—the all-too-familiar double shift. According to exacting local standards, the home itself should be neat and tidy, the children clean and properly dressed. While industrial production of foodstuffs and convenience foods have made appearances into stores in recent years, most Sicilians still appreciate and expect homemade food prepared daily from seasonally available items. All this places a heavy burden on the female members of Sicilian households and spurs a demand for paid domestic labor. At the same time, smaller families and the graying populace has left fewer adult (female) children with the obligation of caring for greater numbers of elderly parents. While this demographic shift is taking place across the country, the way it is addressed varies considerably by locality. In general, southerners and residents of small towns and rural areas throughout Italy stand ready to care for their aged. Retirement homes and assisted-care residences are rare and either prohibitively expensive (in the case of fancy private establishments) in these areas or badges of shame (in the case of church and government-run institutions for the poor). Sicilians feel the impersonal care of nursing homes is only to be relied upon as the last resort by people who care little or not at all for their elderly.

In sum, over the course of the past twenty years increased participation of Sicilian women in higher education and in the labor market, an aging population, rising consumption standards, and insufficient social services have created a vast demand for domestic workers among the middle and upper classes of Palermo. Despite high levels of unemployment and underemployment, Sicilians reject such work as dirty and degrading. Employment as a live-in maid, as we have seen, recalls the servile relations of the past and presents formidable obstacles to family formation. Caring for the elderly is also eschewed as undesirable. It is considered low status due to its association with the home, with women's unpaid work, and with the elderly who are dependent on caretakers for basic needs such as hygiene. Sicilian youth, though suffering unemployment rates approaching 50 percent as a group, refuse to consider domestic work for the same reasons that their peers in the north reject factory jobs. Such work confers a low status and involves much physical effort at inconvenient hours. As Maurizio Ambrosini has pointed out, rejecting these jobs can be seen as rational in the sense that it stems from the recognition that accepting such work, even temporarily, could actually blight one's resumé and harm the search for a desirable job.[18] Small wonder then that immigrants make up the majority of caregivers and lower-level factory workers in Italy.

Like the rich before them, the Sicilian middle class solved the problem of demand by turning to immigrants. For reasons explained in chapter 2, from the late 1980s new and diverse populations arrived in Sicily, swelling the ranks of potential domestic employees. Lacking the connections and experience of the established populations from the Philippines, Mauritius, and Cape Verde, these Ivorians, Ghanaians, Sri Lankans,

Bangladeshis, and others turned for jobs, housing, and other assistance, at least initially, to church organizations, notably the Catholic institutions Santa Chiara and Caritas, and the Protestant Centro Immigrati (CEMI). Typically holding (expired) tourist visas and desperate to support themselves and families back home, they accepted any work they could get, and that usually meant cleaning and caring. In the early to mid-1990s, thousands of foreigners awaiting amnesty provided the city's middle class with a vast supply of cheap and willing servants. Caritas representative Caterina LoCastro described the buyer's market of the day, saying that "every schoolteacher," that is, many middle-class households in Palermo, employed an immigrant at least part-time. The economic crisis of mid-decade, exacerbated by the fallout from investigations into kickback schemes among the political class and a crackdown on organized crime, slackened demand and sent prices tumbling. More than a few employers exploited immigrant vulnerability. The Caritas representative recounted a discussion with a Sicilian woman in which the employer, who was paying a mere 450,000 Lire per month (about US$250) or about half the going rate for full-time service in 1998, inquired whether she could deduct the cost of meals and a bed on those occasions when she required twenty-four-hour coverage. LoCastro exploded, "Madame, Caritas does not condone slavery! Slavery was abolished long ago! If you need her to work longer hours, you should pay her more, not less." Although extreme, this case reflects a widespread sense of entitlement among employers and shows how wages hinge on the employee's knowledge of the market and ability to drive a bargain.

With the long-awaited amnesty of 1995, those who had been all but confined to the city's domestic sector left for the factories, industrial farms, and service sectors of Pordenone, Bergamo, Milan, and other points north. The local economy revived, demand rebounded, and prices rose to former levels. New arrivals, notably from Bangladesh and Sri Lanka at this point, assumed the vacant positions as caregivers and cleaners. The cycle would continue with the amnesties of 1998 and 2002.

MEN IN DOMESTIC SERVICE

In addition to the influx of new nationalities, the domestic market also saw a changing sex composition of workers. Of course, in Palermo as elsewhere domestic work is considered women's work, and foreign women do in fact predominate in the sector.[19] It is also true that numbers of foreign men (and women) secured a permit in the 1995 amnesty by faking domestic employment.[20] Interviews with church volunteers, who often field requests from employers, indicate that immigrant men frequently accept such employment and have since the early 1990s if not before. Indeed, we have rarely encountered an immigrant man who has not, at some time, worked cleaning houses or caring for the elderly. Our impressions are corroborated by a study conducted in 2000 showing that about one-quarter of foreign men interviewed in Palermo work in the sector.[21]

Extremely limited opportunities in other occupations account for the significant presence of men in this traditionally female sector, as the following case shows. John, from Ghana, long knew that emigration could provide financial security. Three of his four siblings live abroad—one sister in New York City, another in Norway, and a brother in northern Italy. Finding himself unable to support his wife and two children on his salary of about US$50 per month at a building supply company, John left alone for Italy. His brother, who works in a pasta factory in Brescia, helped him receive a two-week tourist visa. Not wanting to be a burden to his brother, John stayed in Milan, where he enrolled in an Italian language course and surveyed his chances in Italy. He quickly understood that work and residence in the north required a permit, so he followed many others with expired visas southward where he had heard it was possible to live and work without a permit.

Try as he might, John was unable to obtain employment after his arrival in Palermo in the winter of 2000–2001. As a black man with no knowledge of Italian, his job prospects were dim. He could locate work neither through co-nationals nor the Associazione Pellegrino della Terra (Pilgrim of the Earth Association), a program linked to the Chiesa Valdese (Presbyterian Church). So John went to one of the city's teeming open-air markets, purchased a large backpack, and filled it with cleaning supplies. He then set out door to door, offering his services. Within a few months he had secured work enough to keep him active from 6:30 to 3:00 every day but Sunday; a devout Christian, like most Ghanaians we met, he would never consider working the Sabbath. Each day takes him to another section of the city. He does it all: cleaning stairs, kitchens, even entire apartments.

Another factor channeling men into domestic work is the pressing need for assistance for the elderly. Both the heavy nature of the work and the preference for same-sex attendants has created a demand for male caregivers. Men from Sri Lanka and the Philippines, drawing on strong networks composed of employers and co-nationals with experience in domestic service, cluster in the domestic sector. Others, such as Bangladeshis and West Africans, tend to accept such work in the absence of other employment. Like immigrant women, men complain of long hours, low status, and insecure employment. A few even report sexual advances on the part of employers. Men usually commute to work, though some live with their employer. In the case of a Filipino family of four, the husband lives with his Sicilian employer while his wife and children rent space in the home of co-nationals. The family is reunited twice weekly, Thursday and Sunday evenings, on the husband's time off. Weekday mornings are frantic as the wife prepares the children for school before rushing off to her post as a live-out maid.

YOUNG IMMIGRANTS AND OLD SICILIANS

Immigrants now dominate the live-in market and are a significant presence in the live-out one. Women are generally responsible for house cleaning, washing and ironing clothes, and food shopping. After being trained to cook Sicilian dishes, female domestics are charged with meal preparation and clean-up. Men tend to be assigned outside cleaning, maintenance tasks, moving heavy objects, and washing stairs. While some female live-ins may tend children as part of their chores, few newcomers report working primarily as child minders. Immigrants cannot support themselves on the short hours available and employers prefer to entrust their children to grandparents or, if they must pay, to young Sicilian women who speak Italian fluently.

One of the most common tasks performed by immigrants is caring for the elderly, a pattern that dates to the late 1980s. Immigrant experiences caring for elderly Sicilians vary widely. In some cases the affective relationship endures long after the cessation of the working one. Maria arrived from El Salvador in 1982 and worked for years as a live-in maid. Later, she found her own apartment and worked part-time while pursuing certification for elder care. (With professional pride, Maria observed that she provides the elderly with expert care rather than the simple companionship offered by the mass of immigrant caregivers.) Returning to Sicily from a trip home, she discovered that one of her patients had died. The woman's husband asked her to move in, explaining that he could not bear to eat meals alone after a half century of company at the table. She would have her own room and bath area in the spacious apartment, he assured her. He wanted company, not a worker, he was careful to say, and observed that he would continue to pay for a house cleaner (who turned out to be a more recent female immigrant). Maria hesitated, fearing a loss of autonomy after a dozen years in her own apartment. In the end she moved in and they have both been very happy with the arrangement. "I feel like I've found a father," she said in 2004. The creation of such family-like bonds is probably rare, but this is not the only case we have encountered.

As a rule, the relationship between immigrant caregiver and older Sicilians is a fleeting one. As we have seen, foreigners are mobile and their elderly charges can die. But as short-lived as it may be, the relationship can entail intimacy. Some grown children hire an immigrant to provide company to a parent left lonely by the death of a spouse. Jean, of the Ivory Coast, for example, accompanied an older but self-sufficient widow on errands. He also did some light cleaning and garden work. The woman's son, who had hired him, was so pleased that he referred him to his friends and even hired Jean and his wife to work in his own house.

When the person to be cared for is incapacitated due to age or disease, however, the work can be physically exhausting and involve intimate bodywork and frequent contact with bodily waste. Caring for an invalid involves a daily routine of cleaning, feeding, lifting, and moving, interspersed with slack moments, when the person is asleep or sitting in front of the television. In cases in which the patient is a restless sleeper or requires twenty-four-hour care, immigrants remain the night, assisting and comforting their charges. This work is very demanding, and two immigrants typically coordinate care in such cases.

Immigrants clearly provide a needed service to Sicilian families attempting to cope with the requirements of their elder members. By assuming the dirtiest tasks, they also enable adult Sicilian children to maintain the distance and respect expected in parent-child relations. Research conducted in Greece suggests this is a common motivation for hiring foreign caregivers across southern Europe.[22] Grown children, feeling embarrassment at the prospect of providing intimate care to parents, gratefully hire foreigners to do so. In Palermo, a woman from Cameroon put it differently. She maintained that grown Sicilian children fear touching their parents because they represent death. "They prefer to have a black do the dirty work—as though that will protect them from death!"

The speaker's criticism of Sicilian attitudes toward the elderly was echoed in many conversations with immigrant caregivers. West Africans in particular contrasted their own dutiful and respectful attitudes toward elders with what they regarded as the disrespectful stance adopted by grown Sicilian children toward their own parents. They describe the lives of many older Sicilians in pathetic terms: they live alone, receiving only periodic visits, and must fend for themselves in a fast-paced and demanding world. In his work at a grocery store, a young Cameroonian man often witnesses the pitiful spectacle of older Sicilians struggling to do what a younger person could accomplish with little effort. Earning no wage, Peter makes money by collecting tips for bagging and delivery and by retrieving the 500 Lire coin (the equivalent of about US$.25 in 2001) shoppers must insert to release a shopping cart. One day a frail old man entered the store. Peter bagged his purchases and began to push the cart.

The man was so weak he could muster only a slow shuffling gait. Peter felt great pity for the man as well as disgust at his family:

> He turned to me and said, "Please put me in the trolley." I told him I couldn't do that. It was like he had become a child again. I'm telling you, I don't think he's alive today, really. Imagine making an old man like that go out to fetch his own bottled water for drinking. It's so heavy!

Comments like these bring to the fore culturally embedded expectations of intergenerational relations. One man's loneliness may be another's autonomy. According to Sjaak Van der Geest, Anke Mul, and Hans Vermeulen,[23] people in Ghana look with disfavor on paying an outsider to care for one's elders. In the rare cases in which it does happen, paid care providers are not permitted to perform the intimate bodywork that family members must to do as a form of respect. From the European perspective, grown children struggle to meet expectations of generational reciprocity by exchanging money for care when they cannot provide it themselves. Such an arrangement also enables both parties to retain their independence, a value cherished as much as interdependence in familial relations. The same authors describe how a Greek family came to terms with elder care. A middle-aged woman living in Athens hired a succession of immigrant women to care for her aging parents. When her father died, she considered moving her mother into a facility in the city. In this way her mother would be nearby and receive proper medical attention. Her mother protested these designs, saying she preferred life in her village. The matter was resolved when the Bulgarian nurse who had been attending to the couple agreed to stay on with the mother. Our Sicilian materials suggest that generational balancing acts like this are probably quite common across southern Europe, where old age facilities are rare and viewed with suspicion, and where the practice of hiring domestic servants remains much more prevalent than in the European north.

WAGES, WORKING CONDITIONS, AND RESPECT

Central to the immigrant experience in Sicilian homes is the employer-employee relationship. In theory, employer and employee sign a contract binding them to the collectively bargained, industrywide national contract.[24] The national standards stipulate working conditions, pay, and benefits. A four-tiered pay scale is based on the job description and employee qualifications. The employer is obliged to register the employee and make contributions in her or his name to the national social security program.[25] This gives the employee the right to a series of benefits, including vacation, partially paid sick leave, severance pay, and disability, maternity, and unemployment benefits. Industry standards have improved over time; for example, the maximum hours of work permitted under the 1992 contract is fifty-six per week, down from sixty-six in 1974, the year of the first agreement. In case of employer misconduct, the employee may seek redress with one of the three national unions or, which is more likely, with one of the national associations for domestic workers, ACLI-COLF or API-COLF. Their Palermo offices offer a variety of services, including free legal assistance.

Reality is considerably more complex. Pay and working conditions hinge on a set of factors, including prevailing economic conditions, the pool of available workers, employer requirements and budget, and the immigrant's abilities, legal status, and appearance. Many employers insist on informal arrangements, thereby saving themselves the added expense and legal obligations entailed by a contractual agreement. In some cases, informal arrangements can benefit the immigrant as well. For someone hoping to accumulate the maximum amount of cash before returning to his or her country of origin, the prospect of untaxed income is welcome. In another, more common scenario, lack of permit and hunger compel an immigrant to accept miserable working conditions and undocumented employment.

The domestic sector has become increasingly regularized over the last ten years. Employers now face heavy sanctions for hiring an illegal alien, and immigrants are required to submit proof of employment to retain legal standing. Still, this trend has taken a characteristic turn as many employers register workers and duly submit pension contributions only to reduce wages accordingly, effectively transferring the costs of pension contributions onto the workers themselves. Even with the legal protections afforded by the contract, immigrants remain vulnerable to the depredations of employers. The intimate character of the working relationship, particularly in the case of the live-in position, can give rise to exploitation and abuse. Domestic employers, like their counterparts in other sectors, habitually fall behind in their payments to workers, stringing them along with promises.

Relations with Sicilian employers run the gamut from fleeting to enduring, friendly to bitterly unpleasant. Some describe their relationship with employers as respectful and satisfying; long-term residents who speak the language well are much more likely to have enjoyed such relationships. Others have had such bad experiences that they leave, never to return even to pick up the pay owed them. Most report that employers expect them to do "everything." A woman employed to take care of an invalid mother finds herself cleaning and cooking for the entire family while her charge naps. Or a couple taken on to perform indoor and outdoor tasks, respectively, is asked to stay on for parties for no additional pay. Immigrant women frequently experience the unwanted advances of employers (and other Sicilian men) who regard the women as "hot," that is, as exotic, erotic, and sexually available, as the following story shows.

In the late 1990s, Judith left Ghana for Palermo, where she joined her husband, Richard. Like most foreign women in the city, the only employment she could find was inside Sicilian homes. One of her very first jobs took a nasty turn. The first day her husband accompanied her; resident in Palermo much longer than she, he could navigate both the city and the language. Trouble started when she reported to work the next day. The Sicilian employer followed her throughout the apartment, first patting her bottom, and then making explicit sexual gestures. In her rudimentary Italian, Judith attempted to fend him off, calling him "grandpa" and generally indicating that he was too old for her. Not to be rebuffed, he took up cleaning equipment with vigor and joined her in scouring the apartment. This was his way of displaying his stamina, she conjectured. At the end of the period he offered her the equivalent of US$100 to join him in bed. She refused and never returned.

Foreign domestic workers commonly express frustration at what they see as their relegation to demeaning work and a lack of respect on the part of Sicilians. In 1990 Rebecca left the Philippines for Palermo. She quickly found work through the extensive network of her mother, who had settled in the Sicilian capital the previous decade. In one of her first jobs, she and two other Filipinas cleaned an apartment every week. Once, when she was engaged in a "deep cleaning" of the kitchen, the employer came in and told her to stop. "Just do a little at a time," her employer instructed, "that way you won't get things messed up." Rebecca took umbrage at the suggestion that she was incapable of keeping things straight. As a property owner, skilled worker, and university graduate, she was accustomed to respect back home. But in Palermo she was relegated to the lowly status of cleaner, her performance of even the simplest task scrutinized.

Or consider Esmeralda, the Cape Verdean woman who walked off the job in 1990 because her employer, a Sicilian housewife younger than she, insisted on linguistic deference. The *padrona di casa* wanted Esmeralda to address her with the polite form (*Lei*) but insisted on using the familiar form (*tu*) when speaking to her. "She wants to treat me like a child," complained the immigrant, referring to the way adults use the informal form when speaking to children. Esmeralda, who was fluent in Italian and had citizenship from a marriage (then dissolved) to a Sicilian, felt that working as a servant for a woman her own age was deference enough. She also objected to the low pay offered. This case serves as a reminder that immigrants, while often disadvantaged, can and do refuse what they regard as unacceptable conditions.

THE HIERARCHY

With the expansion of services and personnel, an informal ranking of populations has emerged in the domestic market, with higher status associated with better pay, job security, and benefits. At the top stand Filipinos, followed by Cape Verdeans, Mauritians, South Americans, and Sri Lankans, followed in turn by Bangladeshis, with West Africans firmly at the bottom. In part, this loose ranking reflects of the skills and timing of entry of the diverse populations. Filipinos and other career domestic populations generally speak good Italian, possess legal status, enjoy established networks among employers and co-nationals, and know how to meet employer expectations. Firm institutional support and a thorough understanding of the law further strengthen their ability to negotiate superior wages and working conditions. In contrast, the more recent arrivals typically lack permits, know fewer potential employers, and have to compete with one another for the less desirable part-time work. Many also lack the job skills and professional commitment characteristic of the career domestic populations. According to Sicilian employers, Filipinos are more punctual than Sicilians themselves whereas Ghanaians and Ivorians have an unacceptably casual relationship with the clock.

Combining and conflating skin color, religion, and nationality, the hierarchy also expresses the widespread if rarely stated belief that those who are white, Western, and Christian are more acceptable than, if not superior to, others. This essentialist view, in which whole populations are characterized and judged, is often expressed in the language of race. Filipinos, thoroughly Westernized after a century of heavy U.S. influence, for the most part Catholic, and slightly darker than and physically distinct from Sicilians, are considered "whites." Employers also consider "just like us" the Cape Verdeans, Mauritians, and Sri Lankans, who may be Catholic or Hindus and who are on average much darker than Sicilians. Bangladeshis, another dark South Asian population, are considered undeniably foreign by virtue of their Islamic faith and, for women, distinctive dress. At the same time their deferential "Asian" manner wins them praise from employers.

West Africans, in contrast, are deemed truly "black," a population apart. Church and lay volunteers acting as intermediaries report that employers often express anxiety at the prospect of a "black" in their home. Some claim that their aged parents recoil at the touch of the black hands of their would-be caregivers. Prospective employers commonly inquire about the nationality of a potential worker only to refuse curtly to hire an African. In this respect we should note that, compared to the situation in the United States, in Italy there are fewer restraints, both cultural and legal, on the expression of prejudice. This is evident in printed advertisements as well. In the July 30, 2001 issue of the free weekly, *Giornale delle Pulci*, a request for a live-in domestic specifies a "Filipina or Eastern European girl" and another asks for an Eastern European. A boutique selling ladies' undergarments is looking for a woman, "even of color," while a cleaning job in an office is earmarked for a "helper of color." These views are not lost on Judith, whose unfortunate experience in a Sicilian house was described earlier. She complains that Sicilians regard Africans as good for only the lowest occupations, like cleaning. As proof she points to the case of an ophthalmologist, also from Ghana, who assumed her husband's cleaning job when he departed for the northeast. (Like so many West African men, her husband had sought work in the north once his permit had come through; we return to the question of mobility later.) Although they are Christian and, in the case of those from the Ivory Coast, quick to learn Italian by virtue of their experience with French, West Africans remain at the bottom of a market segmented by race and nationality.

Gender also figures significantly in the stereotypes and experiences that make up the informal ranking. As we have seen, domestic duties are women's responsibilities, and to perform these tasks in the home of another is especially low status, all the more so if the worker is male. Indeed, Sicilian employers were initially skeptical of the abilities of men in this domain but have come to appreciate the skills of foreign men in a variety of endeavors, not the least of which are the care and companionship they offer to infirm and elderly relatives. It is clear that the men did not leave home with the hope of becoming caregivers and cleaners. After all, domestic work ranks at or near the bottom of the occupation ladder in virtually every country. In a scenario common to the immigrant experience, force of circumstances compelled these men to put aside their qualms.[26] With very few exceptions, cleaning and caring were the only options available through friends, newspaper advertisements, and the church centers. For men who joined wives or sisters long resident in Palermo, connections to employers facilitated entry into stable domestic employment. Some Sicilian observers attribute the success of Asian men in domestic service to culture. Asians respect order and cleanliness and so train their children—even the boys!—or so claimed a union official, shaking his head in wonderment. In so doing they cultivate a population of discreetly efficient servants. He attributed the mediocre performance of West African men in the field to lack of concern for order and a grudging acceptance of what they considered women's work.

The case of North African populations, made up overwhelmingly of men, is different. According to observers, Tunisian and Moroccan men have never been offered work in Sicilian homes. The men are said to consider domestic work the province of women and as such far beneath their dignity. The same unionist who described the sense of order of Asian residences characterized the dwellings of North African men as squalid. Re-counting a visit to the home of Tunisian friends, he described declining their kind offer of dinner in order to escape the filth. It is debatable whether the disdain of Arab men for household chores actually surpasses that of their Ivorian and Ghanaian counterparts. It is clear, however, that West Africans are more likely to frequent the church centers that serve as informal employment bureaus for undocumented immigrants. By con-trast, North Africans, by virtue of their networks, have stronger ties to other areas in the service sector (in restaurants and bars, for example), commercial activity, and, in the countryside, to farming. The absence of North African men in Sicilian homes also stems from a long history of conflict and cohabitation between two peoples separated by just under 70 miles of Mediterranean Sea. As Muslims, Tunisians represent historical foes; as single men, their entry into the Sicilian home would provoke dis-comfort; and the widely reported role of Tunisians in petty drug dealing is not likely to go unnoticed by prospective employers. At the same time Sicilians readily acknowledge the profound historical, demographic, and cultural links between the two peoples. In the end, many Sicilians resolve these complexities by insisting on their physical distinctiveness from North Africans, despite a known history of population mixing. Although Tunisians and Sicilian resemble one another physically, and in many ways culturally, much more than do Sicilians and Filipinos or Mauritians, Tunisians are never described as "just like us" or "white."

The hierarchy influences interactions within the workplace and en-gages immigrant identities. The experience of a young Filipina illustrates this dynamic. Rebecca, whose arrival in Palermo in 1990 is described earlier, left her cleaning job for a full-time position caring for an old man with Parkinson's disease. Ranked in the so-called "super" or most skilled category of domestic work, she received a good salary.[27] She and another Filipina shared duties offering round-the-clock care to the man. To com-pensate for what she regarded as demeaning work, Rebecca dressed sharply. The employer was impressed with her work and appearance, and would proudly introduce her to visitors as "doctoressa," an honorific sig-nifying her status as a college graduate. The wife also worked alongside Rebecca in the kitchen and complimented the Filipino dishes she occasionally prepared. Because other immigrants had told us that their employers would never sample exotic fare, we expressed surprise at her success. "You know," she observed, "it's different with us. Filipinos are trusted more than others." In a similar vein, representatives of a Sri Lankan (Tamil) association pointed out that Sicilians feel very comfort-able allowing their female and male compatriots into their homes. "There has never been a case of a Tamil stealing or doing anything wrong," they asserted with pride. In general, those populations at or near the top of the hierarchy tend to celebrate their high status relative to other domestic workers (whether Sicilian or foreign) even as they lament their relegation to a dead-end occupation. Immigrants near the bottom of the hierarchy, on the other hand, are more likely to dismiss the existence of the ranking or to portray Filipinos as clannish snobs. They alternatively cite examples of their own people achieving good positions and complain that employers mistrust and mistreat them as "blacks."[28]

What we have called the hierarchy should not be considered rigid or immutable but rather a fluid classification system and informal set of guidelines shaping and shaped by interactions between diverse immigrant populations and Sicilians. In Palermo, employers wield great power over workers in the domestic realm, as they do in other sectors. A passport from the Philippines and connections to the city's elite may secure access to steady, documented employment. But poor performance will close doors fast, and an inability or disinclination to insist on one's rights can result in low wages and miserable conditions, even for an individual of desirable nationality. In these circumstances a Ghanaian man may make more money than a Cape Verdean woman. Groups also have some room to reposition themselves in the ranking. The movement to points north of many Filipinos, Cape Verdeans, and Mauritians in the course of the 1990s has created space for Sri Lankans and Bangladeshis. And women from North Africa, who have recently begun to arrive in greater numbers than before, have entered the sector. Finally, Sicilian employers differ with regard to how they view groups and the extent to which they view racial categorization as meaningful or legitimate.[29]

This complex set of stereotypes and experience, fluid though they may be, are significant because they inform employer-employee relations and pervade ethnic identities, aspirations, and networks. The operation of the hierarchy powerfully conditions the immigrant condition because immigrant integration hinges on employment and because most jobs involve cleaning and care. As we will see later, it is precisely the limitations of the opportunity structure in Palermo that compel so many to seek stability elsewhere once they have obtained a permit. But first we address the opportunities, challenges, and dilemmas domestic employment entails for immigrant family life.

IMMIGRANT FAMILY LIFE

With few exceptions, the immigrant aims to contribute to his or her family. Unmarried people may emigrate as part of a project to diversify family interests; with the financial backing and moral support of parents and established siblings, they are sent off to stake a claim in the West. Married men or women typically go abroad to support a spouse and children; in the case of domestic workers, women more often than men play the role of the lone sojourner. While their departure is ostensibly about providing for the family, the move can also serve to liberate them from unsatisfactory relationships or domineering fathers. Of course, men may also long to leave a bad situation, but as they have more options at home they need not turn so readily to emigration. In some cases, couples travel together; in this way they share the adventure and can pool earnings earmarked for the maintenance of an extended family at home (in whose care they may have left their own children).

Perhaps the constraint most keenly felt by immigrants is the disruption of family life. Distance from family and spouse can entail loneliness, lapses in child and elder care, disputes over remittances and other financial matters, and the straining and dissolution of relationships. During prolonged separations, not a few immigrants in Palermo have formed new and competing relationships, including children, or found that their partners remaining at home have done so.

The possibilities and exigencies of life abroad can complicate courtship and romance, too. Unions that cross ethnic, religious, or national boundaries may occasion condemnation from co-nationals in Palermo as well as from family members at home. Unofficial marriages are also common, especially when the couple lacks the money or permits to return home. West African and Bangladeshi couples in Palermo often eschew the Italian civil marriage ceremony in favor of a common law union that will, in time, be properly celebrated in the home country. A couple from Ghana, for instance, sent the equivalent of US$200 home to sponsor their wedding held in their absence. On a large-screen television in their dingy apartment in Palermo in 2001, we watched the videotaped ceremony in which family members stood in for the real bride and groom. The Ghanaian woman in Sicily wore the ring that had been blessed in the ceremony while adorning the hand of the surrogate bride.

Children—their presence or absence, upbringing, and future—stand at the core of immigrant family life. Many delay having children until the future. While quite aware of the sacrifices involved, some parents have children in Italy or send for those they have left at home. In addition to the pleasures and responsibilities of parenthood, the couple view raising a child in Italy as an investment in the future. Armed with fluency in Italian and Italian educational credentials, the child will be equipped to climb the socioeconomic ladder. Leaving dirty work far below, she will make her parents proud. Eventually, an Italian passport promises her mobility not just within Italy itself but across the expanse of the entire EU. In this scenario, an adult child might relocate in Germany, France, or the United Kingdom, countries with strong economies, deep immigration histories (including established middle-class communities of foreign origin), and quite possibly links to the homeland of her parents. Moving up often means moving north.

Notwithstanding the compelling force of these hopes, life in Italy undoubtedly sharpens the challenges of parenthood. Raising a family in Palermo, an expense that weighs heavily on many Sicilian parents, places an extraordinary strain of the meager budgets of newcomers. Childcare services in Palermo are few, far between, and often expensive. Some immigrant parents alternate looking after one another's children, and a few immigrant women run small daycare services in their apartments. But at the end of the day, caring for a child reduces the ability of the adult to work for wages, an exchange many can ill afford to make.

In addition to financial sacrifices and the juggling act of work and home duties, raising children in Italy can drive an attitudinal and linguistic wedge between generations. Kids may be embarrassed at their parents' accented Italian, perplexed at their father's or mother's intense concern with a faraway homeland, and chafe at going without the clothes and other items their Sicilian friends enjoy—all in the name of some greater project involving responsibilities to relatives in distant places. For their part, parents watch with dismay as their own flesh and blood adopt the mannerisms, language, and orientations of Sicilian youth. They may fear the influence of the mafia culture that pervades the poor neighborhoods in which so many newcomers reside. Parents also worry that the Italian education system fails to provide adequate training in foreign languages, information technology, and other competencies required for success in the wider world. And life in Italy exposes children to the inevitable racial slurs and taunts on the playground and streets. Increasing numbers of immigrant pupils in Palermo schools and recent efforts on the part of schools and teachers have mitigated, but not eliminated, these problems.

Given these many constraints and dilemmas, many immigrant parents make the painful decision to live apart from their children. A child born in Palermo is sent to live with grandparents or other members of the extended family at home, and those left in the care of relatives at home will remain there. In this way a child will come to appreciate the culture and religion of the homeland, or so the parents reason. In some cases religious concerns dovetail with educational aspirations. The case of a young Bangladeshi couple illustrates this logic. When their son, who had been born in Palermo, reached age five, the wife brought him back to Bangladesh to live with the husband's family. The father explained how the youngster would receive proper instruction in Islam at home and, thanks to the money he earned in Sicily, be able to attend an English-language school. "I speak English with him on the phone now," the father said with pride. He freely acknowledged the painful separation from his family but described it as a necessary sacrifice for the boy's well-being and future. Born in Italy of parents with all their papers in order, the child would be able to return to Europe. The father went on to dream that one day his son would be able to study or work in England where he had several relatives. The father remained alone in Italy in this case, while in others the couple (or the single parent) stays and the child leaves for the homeland. Despite the advantages of the strategy, separation can court serious problems for future parent-child rapport. Such an arrangement also places an inordinate burden on the grandparents who tend to the children and who well may have anticipated receiving rather than offering care in old age.

TIES THAT BIND

While these problems confront virtually all immigrant parents in Palermo, regardless of employment, they assume uncommon force for the single and unaccompanied women who predominate in the domestic sector. Almost without exception, employment as a live-in maid—the rule among the first generation of foreign maids and even today the preference of many employers—involves foregoing, restricting, or delaying family formation. Rarely will an employer permit a servant to bring along a child, let alone additional children or a spouse. The rigorous schedule leaves very little time for a relationship, not to mention the consuming task of parenting. Employers are none too pleased to see servants hosting boyfriends or family members in their homes or, before the advent of the cellular telephone, tying up the telephone lines with personal business. Even if a woman were able to afford to bring a child (or spouse) over to join her, obtaining the requisite permits was extremely difficult in the past and remains a chore today. The cost of providing housing, other necessities, and supervision for a child in Italy is prohibitive.[30] Finally, pregnancy, while supposedly protected by law, results in the loss of work because employers are unwilling to hire a second domestic while the first cares for her newborn.

In the case of the pioneering Cape Verdean, Filipina, and Mauritian maids in the 1970s and 1980s, they in effect sacrificed their own maternal aspirations to provide their female Sicilian employers with greater leisure and the possibility to pursue both career and maternal roles. Among the very first immigrants to Italy, the women were disadvantaged by lack of experience and networks, the overwhelming power of employers, and scant legal protections. Up until the 1986 law, domestic service provided one of the few avenues for documented employment for foreign women. At the same time, ACLI-COLF, the largest national organization for domestic workers, promoted the live-in option for immigrant women. This sponsorship encouraged full-time employment but tended to ignore the devastating effects on immigrant family life of residence with the employer.[31] While the legal protections of immigrants have improved and the understanding of the dilemmas faced by foreign domestics has deepened, the following story shows that even in the contemporary period paid domestic work continues to link immigrant and Sicilian families in an unequal exchange.

Anne Marie left the Ivory Coast at the age of eighteen, leaving her young son in her mother's care. She could not count on the support of the boy's father, who had dropped out of sight during her pregnancy. On the recommendation of a family member, she contacted a Senegalese agent who procured for her a tourist visa for Italy. Late in 1993, she and a cousin took a bus to Ghana, flew to Rome, and journeyed by train down to Palermo. There the women met up with Anne Marie's aunt. In July 1994 Anne Marie obtained a job through Caritas; as a live-in caretaker, she received one million Lire per month (about US$600 at the time). She worked an extraordinarily long week, with time off from Sunday afternoon to Monday morning at 10:00. Her duties included caring for an obese and terminally ill woman as well as cooking for the family and cleaning the house. "The work was so hard I just wanted to quit every day," she remembered. She was so exhausted and anxious that she missed her period for three months and feared for her health.

When the woman died after nine months, Anne Marie agreed to remain in the husband's employ on a live-out basis. Six days a week she cleans, cooks, and irons, from 8:45 to 7:00. The family decreased her monthly salary by twenty percent when they formally declared her as an employee and were required to pay contributions to the national pension fund. While the work is less physically demanding now, it is far from ideal. With his wife dead, the man's temperamental fits have become more frequent; he screams at Anne Marie, blaming her for anything and everything. He refuses to sample the Ivorian food she has prepared. And she is not allowed to take a key with her when exiting the building to pick up needed items. Upon her return from a shopping trip, a family member lowers the key in the basket normally used to haul up goods purchased from ambulant vendors—an operation she finds particularly irritating for the lack of trust it displays.

Anne Marie has not returned to the Ivory Coast since her arrival in 1993. When she can, she does send money to her mother and child; so far she has sent one and a half million Lire (about US$900). Occasionally she considers bringing her son to Italy, but she has made no effort to look into family reunification procedures. She knows from watching other parents struggle that it is very difficult to care for a child and work full-time. Nor can she rely on family for childcare; in 1998, when we interviewed Anne Marie, both her aunt and cousin had relocated in France in search of better possibilities. Another cousin now lives near Milan and is engaged to marry an Italian. For the moment, however, Anne Marie prefers to remain in Palermo where she is a leader of an association run by immigrant women and enjoys friends, a steady job, and a partner. Anne Marie shares an apartment with her boyfriend, an Italian university student whom she met at the Caritas center for immigrants. She describes his family as very open and friendly. He recently graduated and is searching for a job; when that happens, they plan to marry.

Anne Marie's case shows us that her labor was needed by the Sicilian family in order to permit the sick elderly woman to remain at home with her husband and nearby her adult children. Anne Marie left the Ivory Coast in order to better provide for her mother and her child and quite possibly to escape a hopeless future as a young, single mother. In place of day-to-day support for her son and mother, Anne Marie sends money and gifts. Now in Sicily, Anne Marie is engaged in a new stage of family formation. The story of this young woman from the Ivory Coast demonstrates how the Sicilian family can maintain its structure and function as a residential caretaking unit by relying on foreign labor. It also shows how the immigrant's family life is disrupted, as the traditional responsibilities of child- and eldercare can no longer be fulfilled while the breadwinner remains distant, both emotionally and geographically, from her family.

Given the circumstances, live-in domestic workers—today as in the past—delay pregnancy and family formation or leave their children in the care of spouses and family members. Those who leave children behind try to make the rare visit home. Resources permitting, they send back remittances that pay for school tuition and books, land purchases and home improvements, televisions and refrigerators. They salve the pain of separation and ennoble their hard work by representing it as a necessary sacrifice for the family. At the same time they can take a measure of satisfaction in the way their contributions raise their stature within both their families and their home community.[32] And like Anne Marie, they can realize a freedom of movement and expression in Sicily that may not have been possible at home.

The relationship of women to the children they leave behind, of course, varies enormously. Some women and children communicate frequently, others less so. Some children are abandoned by their mothers, or perceive the separation in these terms. Some children harbor no intention of coming to Palermo while others follow their mother's route to Sicily once they have come of age.[33] In other cases, a mother will endeavor to bring some or all of her children to Italy as soon as she can manage it. A Mauritian woman, Claudine, answered an advertisement in a local newspaper in 1975, the year her husband died. She received an airline ticket from an eager Sicilian employer and, leaving her children in the care of her mother, boarded a plane for Italy. For years she saved the salary she earned as a maid in Mondello, a fashionable seaside resort near Palermo. In time she established an independent residence and sent for all seven of her children. Through hard work and much patience, many of the pioneers of domestic service, like Claudine, were eventually able to secure the lodgings and live-out work necessary for the pursuit of a full family life.

Men, who have increasingly entered domestic labor, also serve to maintain Sicilian households even as they forego the pleasures of family life. Recall the case of John, the enterprising Ghanaian cleaner described earlier. His labor assists diverse Sicilian families in household maintenance while he, an undocumented immigrant, works for little and endures a painful separation from his own family. To save money, he shares an apartment with three other men from Ghana and accepts food from a church center. On his meager salary, John routinely sends several hundred dollars home each month via Western Union. His wife pays the bills and uses the extra money to invest in items for sale in local markets. Through his remittances John hopes to build his family's long-term financial stability. He describes separation from his wife and daughters as very painful. At the end of each month, after he has paid his bills and sent off money to Ghana, he permits himself a telephone call home. The next day he visits the Associazione Pellegrino, recounting with pleasure every turn of the conversation. While proud of what he has accomplished against formidable odds, John admits that he is tired. "I cannot continue at this pace forever. I have to think of the future." He sets his hopes on another amnesty and the opportunity that legal status would grant him to follow others northward in search of steady factory work. Perhaps then he could bring his family to settle in Italy.

GEOGRAPHICAL AND OCCUPATIONAL MOBILITY

Domestic employment, the principal pursuit of immigrants in Palermo, encompasses many activities and offers a wide range of pay, benefits, and job security. Overall, the sector promises lateral rather than vertical mobility and the role of servant epitomizes low status; working conditions, especially for live-in maids (and butlers), impede a full family life. With few alternatives, most immigrants have found themselves compelled to accept such dirty work. As they gain experience, permits, and connections, newcomers strive to improve their situation. Stable employment, dignity, and the possibility of family formation hinge, for most, on occupational mobility, geographic mobility, or both. While every individual presents a unique story, mobility patterns are closely linked to sex and nationality.

Given their limited opportunities in other fields, many women remain in domestic service. Practicing a lateral mobility, they change employers in a search for better pay, benefits, and working conditions. As a live-out maid they may start a family or bring over a spouse or child; and higher pay and steady contributions to the national pension system allow them to balance the household budget and promise future security. While some women stay in Palermo, others have moved to Rome, Milan, and other parts to improve their situation. Employment as a full-time maid in the north means a significant jump in pay, with no corresponding rise in expenses—as long as one resides with the employer. Such a move can also be motivated by personal motives, for example, the desire to be close to a family member or close friend resident elsewhere.[34] Interviews with immigrants and discussions with union and church officials suggest that by the late 1990s a good number of the early arrivals from the Philippines, Cape Verde, and Mauritius had made the journey up the peninsula and in some cases abroad.[35]

Businesses catering to immigrants offer some foreign women a way out of domestic employment. With their knowledge of Italy, language skills, and experience, former domestics can make valuable additions to the phone centers, restaurants, travel agencies, and other enterprises that have flourished from the late 1990s. Juggling domestic work and study, other women have earned certification in fields such as geriatric care, physical therapy, and intercultural communication. Certification allows them to work anywhere in Italy, and qualified personnel are in great demand in some areas of the north. Some do leave in search of employment, citing with irritation the difficulties of landing a job in an area with high unemployment and a society in which connections rather than skills open doors to good jobs. Others elect to stay. They have friends here, their family may be settled, and they call Sicily home now. They also make a decent living, given Palermo's low cost of living relative to the north and the standard pay scale for public sector employment regardless of location. Other women leave domestic work through marriage, especially to an Italian. Intermarriage rates are low and usually involve the union of Italian men and foreign women, often from Mauritius or Cape Verde.

A few women, like Elizabeth, start their own businesses. In 1989, at the age of twenty-five, she left Mauritius to seek her fortune in the world and to support her parents and seven siblings. "My parents didn't want me to leave, I was the oldest girl. But I fought for my future." She was attracted to Palermo both by the presence of a friend and by the reputation of Sicily as an easy place to obtain a permit. As she related with pride in 2001, she landed her first job within two weeks. Like virtually all co-nationals in Palermo, she worked in domestic service. For years she struggled, living alone in a small apartment, saving as much as possible. With time she managed to send money home; in 1996 she brought over a brother who would also find work as a domestic. For her part she limits herself to cleaning, an aversion that may stem from her father's long-time employment as a cook in a French household in Mauritius. Regarding domestic work as degrading, she sought a way out, and after seven years she managed to realize the longtime desire of going to school. She worked one job mornings and another afternoons while going to school evenings. With her diploma and savings, Elizabeth was able to open a beauty shop catering other immigrant women. (Italian shops, she observes, just do not understand how to handle the hair and skin of black clients.) Elizabeth is now able to support herself and her husband as well as send contributions to her family in Mauritius.

To a much greater extent than women, immigrant men regard domestic employment as a refuge activity and seek to leave the sector at the earliest possible opportunity. Newcomer men, like women, would prefer to stay in Sicily. But as we have seen, work outside the home is hard to come by and retaining legal status is a chore, as Sicilian employers are loath to register foreign employees. Permits in hand, immigrant men have streamed to the factories, industrial farms, and the cities of the Italian north and, in some cases, abroad. In this way the Ivorians, Ghanaians, Bangladeshis, Tunisians, and other male-led foreign populations have left Palermo, making room for new arrivals. It is our impression that nearly all male immigrants in possession of a permit have either left the city or are contemplating doing so. (Perhaps a case apart, Sri Lankan families have sought above all entrance to England and Canada, the most populous centers of the Tamil diaspora.)

The move north, it is hoped, will provide the financial and legal security, dignity, and material foundation requisite for the pursuit of a full family life. The move itself, however, frequently entails separation. In a common scenario, permit in hand a man journeys north, finds work in a factory, and lives for some time with co-ethnic men. His wife (and children) remains in Palermo, where the low cost of living, support of friends and relatives, and the possibility of domestic work do not cut into his salary. Once the man has accumulated sufficient funds and secured accommodations of his own—not an easy task given the housing shortage and reluctance of homeowners to rent to immigrants in many areas—his family joins him.

It appears that the move, as difficult as can be, can in fact support family formation. In 2002 we visited Ivorians, formerly of Palermo, who had relocated in an industrial district north of Milan. Starting in the mid- to late 1990s, the men had learned of the area from acquaintances and relatives from Palermo and used these networks to obtain employment in the ubiquitous factories producing metal products. With time, most single men established families while married ones were joined by their wives and children. Interviews, visits to homes, and attendance at a meeting of an Ivorian association all pointed to significant numbers of recent marriages and childbirths. Not surprisingly, plans for a daycare center were afoot. The men (and a few women), who together with southern Italians form the backbone of local industry, point with pride to the salary and benefits they earn even as they smart from the heavy physical labor and long hours. They are keenly aware that, given the provisions of recent immigration law linking the right to residency to documented employment, an economic downturn could wash away the foundations upon which they have built families. They know that they or more probably their wives could always find (undocumented) work caring and cleaning in Palermo, but they are just as certain that they are no longer willing to live without permits and insurance. While these lines are based on a single locality in the north, discussions with immigrants and institutional representatives suggest a strong association between the stable employment and family formation among newcomers.

FAMILY SUBSIDIES

This chapter has explored aspects of Sicilian and immigrant family life as they intersect in a robust domestic labor market. In the past three decades, more and more Sicilians have hired others to do tasks previously covered by family members. With the diversification and expansion of demand for paid domestic labor, thousands of foreign women and men have assumed the roles of servants, cleaners, and caretakers. Immigrants, especially the undocumented and vulnerable among them, in fact safeguard the stability of Sicilian families. At the same time, this important if unacknowledged effort often forces immigrants to alter, delay, and forego their own family plans. While the exigencies of work in Sicily stand in the way of a full family life for all immigrants, the nature of live-in employment all but denies such a pursuit. In a bitter irony, the foreign women making up the majority of live-in maids sacrifice their own maternal careers to play a supporting role to the consumption, family, and career aspirations their Sicilian employers.

Trends toward smaller, longer-lasting families and the dramatic increase in the numbers of dependent elderly present difficult challenges to families across southern Europe. Federica Dell'Orto and Patrizia Taccani's description of Italy holds for Spain and Portugal as well: "The family is overloaded with responsibilities, without almost any compensation, and it reacts by closing in upon itself, seeking a kind of self-sufficiency, which is, however, precarious."[36] Viewed from this perspective, the mass arrival of immigrants in the late 1980s and early 1990s allowed southern European families to cope with heavy burdens by tapping the precarious lot of newcomers. Given an aging populace and the unlikelihood of state intervention in social services in the near future, southerners will continue to hire immigrants to perform tasks traditionally allotted to family members.

While immigrant women (and men) offer home-based care across southern Europe, in northern Europe and the United States they work in old-age facilities, too. Writing of the surging demand for eldercare across the West, William Christian Jr. notes:

> Specialized long-distance migratory streams have formed to make this possible. Once there were streams of rural nursemaids and nannies for the children of the wealthy; now there are multiple streams of elder-nannies to "developed" countries. What are the implications of this trade for the caregivers themselves, and who is caring for their families? The small nuclear families of the first world have a high human cost in care that is "subsidized" by extended families elsewhere.[37]

As the stories of domestic workers so poignantly demonstrate, the human costs of this unacknowledged subsidy are high indeed.

NOTES

1. Official figures confirm our impression that domestic work is by far the most common occupation of immigrants; in 2002, 82 percent of permit-holding foreigners in the province of Palermo worked as domestics, compared with an islandwide average of 56.6 percent and a national one of 48.6 percent (Caritas di Roma 2003: 493). For reasons explained in notes 16 and 17, the figure is probably high.

2. Caritas di Roma 2002: 296–97.

3. For 1991, rates of female labor force participation were 35 percent (Palermo), 46 percent (Rome), 50 percent (Milan), 60 percent (Bordeaux), 63 percent (Frankfurt), and 70 percent (Copenhagen). This information comes from "Urban Audit," a study of over fifty cites in the European Union, sponsored by the Directorate-General for Regional Policy at the European Commission.

4. The figures come from Bacci 2000: 227.

5. Figures for the Greek case come from Mestheneos and Triantafillou 1993: 135; those regarding nursing homes in Italy come from Carbonin et al. 1997: 1520–21; and numbers for aged Italians come from Dell'Orto and Taccani 1993: 114.

6. Accounts include Andall 1998, 1999, 2000a, 2000b; Anderson 2000; Anthias and Lazaridis 2000; Campani 2000; Pugliese 1998; Tacoli 1999; and Zontini 2002.

An interesting contrast with current trends is Brettell's (1995) analysis of the lives and working conditions of Portuguese women in Paris in the 1970s.

7. In particular we have consulted Schneider and Schneider 1976, 1996.

8. While historical studies tend to focus on co-residential servants, we include domestic workers residing with employers as well as those who lived with their own families—probably a common occurrence in the densely nucleated settlements of the Sicily. We cannot offer a percentage of peasant women involved in the sector, but the number was certainly high in the latifundist western part of Sicily; virtually all aristocratic and gentry (*civile*) households hired servants, and artisans and medium-sized farmers hired occasional domestic labor (Jane and Peter Schneider, personal communication, September 2005). According to Giovanna DaMolin (1990), a somewhat different pattern obtained in the center-north of Italy, where young men and women commonly lived and worked with families of farmers and artisans. In this context domestic employment was more a common life stage than a stigma.

9. Schneider and Schneider 1996: 240.

10. Sicily achieved regional status in 1946. Chubb (1982) and Schneider and Schneider (2003) describe the "sack" of Palermo.

11. ACLI-COLF is the acronym for the Associazione Christiane Lavoratori Italiana-Collaboratrici Familiari, the division of the Italian Christian Workers' Association devoted to domestic workers, or *colf*.

12. API-COLF is the acronym for Associazione Professionale Italiana-Collaboratrici Familiari, the Italian Professional Association of Family Helpers.

13. For more detail, see Andall 2000a: 88–112.

14. According to the research of Andall (2000a: 125; 1999: 243), Capuchin friars initiated the immigration of Cape Verdean women to Rome in the late 1960s; for a time they served as informal recruiters for domestic workers, linking prospective domestic workers to Italian families through parish priests in Rome.

15. Andall (1999, 2000a) has described the life and times of women from Cape Verde and East Africa in those years.

16. In interviews conducted in 1990, representatives for ACLI-COLF reported receiving about 1,200 requests for job placements annually while representatives for API-COLF reported about 1,000; in both cases foreign women made up the majority of workers hired.

17. Sicilian female labor market participation in Palermo rose from 28.8 percent in 1981 to 34.7 percent in 1991. These rates remain, however, far below those registered in areas to the north (see note 3).

18. Ambrosini 2001.

19. In a study conducted in 1997 among nearly 400 immigrant women living in Palermo, fully 82.7 percent of those employed earned a living in the domestic sector, broadly defined (Extra 1998, V 24).

20. This regularization, unlike the amnesties of 1986 and 1990, required proof of employment. Some foreigners, among them numbers of North African men who never work as domestics, faked domestic employment, paying an Italian for a bogus contract and making the required social security payments themselves. This trend was particularly pronounced in Sicily (Reyneri 1998; Zincone 2001: 335; 345–46). Nationally, from 1995 to 1996 the number of non-EU workers registered

as domestics soared from just over 59,000 to almost 110,000 (Caritas di Roma 2000: 277). In a similar way many men enter the country under the provisions for domestic employment but do not pick up their permits at state employment offices (Reyneri 1998).

21. For more on the study, see Zincone 2001: 519. The trend also appears to hold in Catania, Sicily's second largest city (Scidà and Pollini 1993: 165–66). It is an open question whether the trend holds nationally. In 1999, men made up over 22 percent of the non-EU citizens registered as domestic workers in Italy (Caritas di Roma 2002: 297). These figures can be misleading in two ways: they understate by failing to capture undeclared employees, and they overstate because numbers of foreigners, particularly males, have faked domestic employment as a means to obtain legal status, as described in the previous note.

22. This observation is made in Van der Geest, Mul, and Vermeulen 2004.

23. See Van der Geest, Mul, and Vermeulen 2004.

24. The relevant sections of the three national (and federated) unions, CGIL, CISL, and UIL, are the signatories for labor while representatives for ACLI-COLF and API-COLF are present for negotiations. Andall (2000a) recounts the history of the contract and the role played by the domestic workers' associations.

25. The Istituto Nazionale della Previdenza Sociale (National Institute of Social Security) provides pensions and offers disability, unemployment, and other benefits to most workers in the public and private sectors.

26. Andall (2000a: 220–21) found that Cape Verdean and East Africans in Rome considered the (rare) entry into domestic labor on the part of co-national men most inappropriate. She recounts how a teenage boy, who lived in a residential home because both parents worked as live-ins, burned with shame at the thought of his father's humiliation.

27. The salary was nearly 1,000,000 Lire per month, just over US$800 at the time.

28. Andall (2000a: 169) notes that other studies have identified Filipinas as the most sought after in the Rome area but seems to question this ranking, citing the opinion of women from Cape Verde and East Africa that they, too, are respected as workers.

29. This is explored in detail in Cole 1997.

30. Andall (2000a) reports Cape Verdean and East African female single parents and couples occasionally placing children in church residential centers or, more rarely, in foster homes.

31. The role of ACLI-COLF is described in detail by Andall (2000a, 2000b).

32. In her study of Filipino women in Rome, Tacoli (1999) found that women wielded their newfound influence within the family to promote the immigration of female rather than male relatives. Women found employment more easily than men, were more inclined to share tasks, and were less likely to become a burden. Favaro (1993) outlines several types of female immigrant family situations.

33. Some young women who have grown up at home may in time exchange positions with their mothers who work as domestics in Italy in what Chell (2000: 118) calls "intergenerational, sequential migration."

34. Andall (2000a: 129–30) describes how Antonia, from Cape Verde, arrived in Palermo in 1977 but moved to Rome a year later to be near her mother who was

working there as a live-in. Antonia made the move by finding a family that was about to relocate to the Eternal City.

35. The northward movement of domestics engenders a chain migration of its own, as observed in the previous note. Such network-driven flows can assume international dimensions as well. Andall (1999, 2000a) describes the movements of Cape Verdean women through Cape Verde, Portugal, Italy, and the Netherlands.

36. Dell'Orto and Taccani 1993: 110.

37. Christian 2000: 120.

4

~

The Food Chain

If nearly every immigrant residing in an urban area has worked inside a Sicilian home, most newcomers in the countryside are engaged in agricultural pursuits. Foreigners tend flocks of sheep, make up the crew of Mazara's large fishing fleet, harvest grapes and olives and oranges, and quarry stone. Like their counterparts in the cities, these immigrants typically journey to Europe and secure a bed and a job there through networks. Agricultural laborers, like domestic workers, render a vital contribution to Sicily while being relegated to the dirtiest tasks and the margins of society. The two populations differ in important respects, however. Tunisians dominate the agricultural workforce whereas many nationalities participate in domestic service. While significant numbers of foreign men now clean house and take care of elderly Sicilians, female agricultural laborers remain a rarity. Finally, differences in the availability of work influence residential patterns and family relations. The domestic sector offers the promise of steady work and promotes long-term residence in Italy whereas the seasonal demand for labor and proximity of North Africa mean that many Tunisian men regard their stays in Sicily as short-term, money-making trips. And whereas Tunisians prefer to leave children and wives at home, immigrant domestic workers are more inclined to form families in Italy—despite the obstacles and the tendency move out of the sector and beyond Sicily.

This chapter takes us across the island, some 150 miles southeast from Palermo to the province of Ragusa.[1] We focus on trends in two settlements at the epicenter of greenhouse cultivation, Vittoria (population circa 55,000) and Santa Croce Camerina (population circa 9,000). The area offers a powerful vantage point onto the indispensable role of immigrant workers in one of Sicily's most productive provinces. The intensive production system demands a great deal of labor, and as the island's largest greenhouse district, the area is home to a large and growing foreign population. At the same time, seasonal labor demand and the prevalence of short-term permits have given a temporary quality to immigrant life. As we shall see, the local contexts of reception have established a kind of social wall between the two populations—one that few on either side are willing to breach. A recent trend toward family formation and the beginnings of an ethnic community are now emerging from the shift to year-round cultivation (and therefore employment), the possibility of renting farmland, and the growing sentiment among long-resident foreigners that their family's destinies will be played out in Italy. A second generation raised in Italy entails particular challenges for North African parents and raises the question of the eventual participation of grown children in a segmented economy and society.

THE EUROPEAN CONTEXT

As was the case for the domestic sector, the situation of immigrant farm workers in Vittoria-Santa Croce[2] is best appreciated in light of the wider context. Agriculture in Europe is very big business. Farmers, who struggled to feed their compatriots in the aftermath of World War II, today produce mountains of excess food and export it throughout the world. Agriculture accounts for nearly half of the European Union's nearly 100 billion Euro annual budget. In Europe as in the United States, recent decades have witnessed a steady decline in the number of people engaged in agriculture along with an astounding rise in productivity. For landowners, farming, at least as a full-time occupation, carries more risks than rewards. Fewer Europeans find farm work attractive or necessary; the local poor, students, and housewives who once harvested grapes or olives can now eschew such temporary, dirty, and low-status employment. Lacking the family and local networks and state supports enjoyed by nationals, and deeply in need of work, any work, to survive and save money, men from North Africa and Eastern Europe assume the most arduous jobs in agriculture and accept substandard wages and conditions, as the case of Tunisians in Vittoria and Santa Croce will show. According to official figures, which are certainly low, foreigners accounted for at least 10 percent of a total EU seasonal workforce of over five million in 2000.[3]

Despite the paucity of material on the phenomenon,[4] existing studies and annual reports issued by national and international institutes reveal patterns. Foreigners in rural Europe are unevenly distributed. They cluster in areas devoted to labor-intensive crops, particularly fruits, vegetables, and flowers, and are scarce in regions specializing in crops, like cereals and potatoes, that permit mechanized cultivation. Immigrants are almost all young and unaccompanied men. Their numbers increase at harvest time and they typically move from crop to crop within an area or from one region to another in pursuit of the next harvest. Greenhouse cultivation, fishing, and animal husbandry, because they require considerable labor inputs year-round, foster instead relatively stable newcomer populations.

Like their peers in the United States, European fruit and vegetable growers face stepped-up international competition and have sought to reduce costs through recourse to a population of semilegal foreigners. The corresponding declines in pay and working conditions make such work less appealing to native workers.[5] Farmers' reliance on foreign farm workers goes beyond desperately needed hands and cost savings. The very fact of immigrant availability also influences crop selection and investment decisions. For example, over the past two decades growers in the Spanish regions of Catalonia and Andalusia have shifted from cereal crops to more labor-intensive fruit trees and greenhouse cultivation. While the potential profitability of the new crops spurred the change, subsequent rapid expansion was made possible by the availability of African workers, mostly from nearby Morocco. Once present, the immigrants become indispensable to the profitability of the system.[6]

EU states, like the U.S. government, also play an important part in the continuing segmentation of the agricultural labor market. Some government officials and politicians routinely call for more restrictive measures. But in reality, tolerance of a large undocumented foreign population together with lax enforcement of restrictive laws, especially in agricultural areas with seasonal imperatives for extra labor, facilitate the widespread use if not outright exploitation of foreigners made vulnerable by need and precarious legal status.[7]

These trends are all in evidence in Italy, one of Europe's most important agricultural producers. Agricultural production remains important in some center-north areas, notably Trentino–Alto Aldige, Veneto, Emilia–Romagna, and Lazio, and in most of the south where it includes about 10 percent of the workforce.[8] Yet, here too the percentage of the local labor force dedicated to the sector has dropped precipitously, from 43.9 in 1950 to 5.3 in 2000.[9] In 1998–1999 alone the number of agricultural employees dropped by 67,000, or 5.6 percent. As Italians have abandoned the sector, foreigners have entered it, though at a slower rate. According to the Italian National Institute for Agricultural Economics, an estimated 92,000 immigrants labored in the country's fields and vineyards in 1999.[10] Most come from North Africa with increasing numbers from Eastern Europe, and over half work in the south. Working conditions, particularly below Rome, can be brutal. Unremitting toil under a scorching sun, squalid accommodations, the labor-boss system, the animosity of local residents, and the presence of organized crime have made the tomato harvests in southern Italy a living symbol of the heartless exploitation of immigrants.

While the situation has improved in recent years, many immigrants still engage in *lavoro nero*, or undocumented work, particularly in the south. Overall, non-EU workers represented about 8 percent of all agricultural workers in Italy in 1999.[11] For reasons described later, these figures certainly underestimate the reliance of farmers (and ultimately of consumers) on immigrant labor. Alongside the recent imposition of stricter border controls, the Italian state has introduced a new category of visa for seasonal work. While workers in tourism receive some of these permits, agricultural laborers, particularly in the northern regions, receive most of them.[12] The annual announcement of the program, which issued about 60,000 visas for 2003 alone, is regularly applauded as essential by Coldiretti, an important national association for growers.

ORIGINS AND DEVELOPMENT OF THE
GREENHOUSE SYSTEM IN SOUTHEASTERN SICILY

While small in size, the province of Ragusa is an agricultural power-house.[13] Out of a provincial population of just under 300,000, more than 20,000 are directly engaged in agriculture and perhaps another 80,000 find work in related fields like transportation, equipment and supplies, packing and processing, and technical assistance. The preeminence of the sector is due in part to the thriving dairy industry on the rocky *altopiano*, or plateau, that descends in giant irregular steps toward the sea. Along the coastal plain, vineyards, cultivated fields, and greenhouses push up against settlements, crowd the narrow roadways, and overlook the Mediterranean Sea. Greenhouse cultivation in particular drives the local economy, accounting for much of the province's wealth.[14]

While new materials and formats are constantly developed, the typical greenhouse today remains a simple, unheated structure composed of wooden framing and plastic sheeting, perhaps graced by a rustic wooden cross. Farms are crammed with greenhouses in various states of repair, and a trip down any rural road promises a vista of plastic and green. Paolo Aquila, a CGIL[15] union official in Santa Croce, called greenhouses "our industry," with all the good and bad the analogy suggests. The ubiquitous structures stand as proof of residents' work ethic and have brought unprecedented wealth to what was once a poor area. At the same time the system entails environmental hazards and blights the countryside, particularly in August when the plastic is removed and rubbish burned in smelly open fires in preparation for the fall growing season. A steady stream of farm vehicles and heavy trucks clogs the area's narrow roads, billowing exhaust and contributing to accident tolls. "Once we could have placed our bet on tourism," Aquila said in reference to the many nearby ancient Greek sites, "but that time has passed."

Vittoria serves as the unofficial capital of greenhouse agriculture. Officials estimate that hothouse products account for nearly 80 percent of the city's considerable wealth. Each day farmers bring tons of produce to the city's vast market, where fruits and vegetables are bought and sorted, sold, packed, and shipped. In a trend spearheaded by the larger farms, instead of going to the city market, goods are now being prepared for shipment in packinghouses; the produce is then trucked directly to big Italian and European distributors in major urban areas in accordance with annual contracts. Neighboring Santa Croce, though only a fifth of the size of Vittoria, boasts its own considerable market and an increasing number of packinghouses.

More than a mere economic or technological fact, the rise of greenhouse cultivation represents a profound social and cultural transformation. Poverty, political repression, and antagonistic class relations between absentee owners of vast estates and land-poor and landless peasants spurred cycles of emigration and peasant political mobilization from the late nineteenth century. In the postwar period, peasants gained unprecedented access to land through sales, sharecropping arrangements, and land reform.[16] These former day laborers turned owners and sharecroppers experimented with ways to make their small parcels render. Pioneers in the Vittoria–Santa Croce area discovered that crops planted in the sandy soil, protected from the elements and nourished by well water, produced yields two to three times as large as those in open fields. Vittoria mayor Francesco Aiello has emphasized the collective quality of this development. Agricultural workers could draw on their experience with intensive techniques, including attempts to grow tomatoes and other vegetables in open fields (as opposed to small and protected gardens) in the immediate postwar period. Erecting crude walls and a roof out of plastic sheeting and wood followed naturally from the traditional use of prickly pear leaves and other plant material to protect young plants from the unrelenting wind. Sharing information and a desire to get ahead, thrifty peasants built an extremely productive and profitable system out of the cheapest of materials. With the new system they could produce more and fetch higher prices for early crops.[17]

Greenhouses proliferated in the 1960s and 1970s. In 1964, the first funds from the regional government arrived for the construction of greenhouses. The same year, Pietro Gentile and other pioneers established

"Rinascita" in Vittoria. This cooperative, which permitted farmers to increase both quality and quantity and distribute their produce more widely, has served as a model for cooperatives in Santa Croce and elsewhere. Greenhouse crops, especially the form of cherry tomato developed locally, sold so well they became known as "green gold." Now assured of the profitability of the system, banks extended loans. Within a decade, thousands of farmers and would-be farmers entered the contest, whether as owners, sharecroppers, or renters. To expand greenhouse acreage, they trucked away sand dunes, leveled the coastal plain, and uprooted carob, olive, and almond trees. Thus was fashioned the "transformed strip" (*la fascia trasformata*) of coastline, more than eighty kilometers stretching from Scoglitti to Pachino in the neighboring province of Siracusa.

The greenhouse system, forged by thousands of peasant entrepreneurs, grew with sporadic government assistance.[18] In Palermo, the regional government, dominated by the conservative Christian Democrats,[19] produced a string of supports such as subsidized plastic sheeting, thanks to the presence of Ragusa natives in positions of power in the department of agriculture. Not forthcoming, however, was systematic attention to chronic problems, such as poor transportation, lack of coordination, and

Photo 4.1.   Greenhouses fill the horizon, Vittoria

Photo 4.2.   Ad for Portobello tomatoes, Vittoria

Photo 4.3.   Farm, Vittoria

underdeveloped distribution channels, so often noted by local Communist and Socialist[20] politicians and unionists. Local leftist administrations,
long a feature in the area, supported the emerging class of small and
medium-sized farmers. In the late 1970s and early 1980s, markets were established in Vittoria and Santa Croce to facilitate the distribution of produce far beyond Sicily.

Proliferation of greenhouses and improved techniques spurred an economic boom in the 1970s and 1980s. Vittorese, with growing profits, purchased more consumer goods. They built bigger houses and appointed
them in a manner befitting their elevated status. They bought new farm
machinery and faster cars; ignoring the blight of greenhouses, they built
second homes in the countryside and along the coast. Still haunted by
memories of poverty and humiliation, the new class of farmers insisted
that their children remain in school and obtain an education that would
permit them to escape the hard and dirty life on the farm. While other
provincial towns and cities were dwindling, Santa Croce grew impres-
sively, from 7,120 in 1950 to 9,125 in 2000.[21]

Farming is a difficult business. Powerful windstorms can damage
greenhouses and frosts can harm the young plants, setting back production. In addition to these perennial concerns, foreign competition, espe-

cially from southern Spain, and rising costs created what observers call a "crisis" in the late 1980s and early 1990s. Today, an integrating and expanding EU together with global markets for foodstuffs continue to bedevil growers. "Vittoria is living through globalization," commented Giovanni Formica, the city's alderman for agriculture, in 2003.[22] He described how the larger enterprises of Vittoria have adapted most successfully by adopting a proactive stance toward the market. A few have tried—without much success—to establish operations in Tunisia and other nearby countries offering significantly lower production costs. Some have sought to meet rising demand for quality products, especially organic ones. Rather than sell their goods at the public market, many farmers now utilize packinghouses and deal directly with distributors and supermarket chains. By stipulating product price, quantity, and quality, such arrangements afford the farmer greater security and permit better advance planning. But as several local firms have learned, failure to meet contractual standards can have serious consequences, including loss of future contracts. For the numerous small and medium-sized farmers, the sea change has proven hard to navigate. In a move the city supports, some have established growers' associations, constructed packinghouses, and forged links with the big outside distributors that dominate the market. In this way, they hope to facilitate planning and secure superior access to distant markets. But most farmers continue to cultivate as they deem fit and bring their goods to market daily. While they smart at declining prices, they are reluctant to part with the routines that for the last thirty years have secured them a good livelihood and an identity as independent producers. Rather than submit to the dictates of a big firm and the regulations of foreign markets, they prefer to retain their hard-won autonomy. But to survive if not prosper, they too must turn to foreign workers.

FOREIGN FARM WORKERS

In the early years of greenhouse cultivation, labor demands were met by farming families and by the Sicilian day laborers who still gathered before dawn in local squares. As additional land went under plastic in the 1970s, farmers turned to nearby areas in the interior. Today, Sicilians continue to gain a livelihood from agriculture but they rarely rub shoulders with foreigners as equals; Sicilians either have skilled positions in larger establishments or they hire immigrants to work on their own farms. Foreign workers now dominate the ranks of common laborers and are indispensable to the continued competitiveness of the area. Criticizing the effects on growers of the restrictive 2002 Bossi-Fini

7

Chapter 4

law on immigration, Vittoria's mayor Aiello stated plainly, "We need immigrants like we need bread."[23]

Following harvests along the island's southern flank, Tunisian men arrived in the Vittoria area in the early 1980s. Discovering that greenhouses afforded more stable employment than open-air agriculture, men began to call relatives, friends, and neighbors. In addition to the continued influx of Tunisians (who still make up 80 percent of the foreign population), the 1990s saw the arrival of Algerians, Albanians, and Moroccans. In recent years Poles and other Eastern Europeans have joined the ranks of greenhouse workers. The number of permit holders in the province has surged from just over 3,000 in 1994 to an estimated 12,000 in 2003.[24] The greenhouse belt, with its enormous appetite for labor, is home to most of the province's foreigners. In 2002, Vittoria and Santa Croce alone counted about 3,000 and 1,000 permit holders, respectively. Union and city spokespeople estimate the actual foreign population is closer to 5,000 for Vittoria and 1,500 for its neighbor, bringing the percentage of foreigners here far above the Sicilian (and Italian) average.[25] Men outnumber women by a ratio of five to one, a pattern in keeping with the demands of agriculture work and Tunisian emigration trends.

The means of arrival and legal status vary across and within immigrant populations engaged in agriculture. Some arrive aboard ships originating from Tunisian ports; despite frequent landings of smugglers' boats along the coastline, the number of people arriving illegally is probably small owing to stepped-up surveillance. Also few are the arrivals authorized under the family reunification provisions of immigration law. By far the majority enter Italy (or Europe) legally, overstay their tourist visa, and have received (or hope to receive) legal status through one of the periodic amnesty programs for which Italy is well known. This pattern is reflected in sharp increases in permit holders following amnesty years.[26] Nationality also conditions the selection of a path to Europe. From about 2002, growing numbers of Poles have arrived in Ragusa on tourist visas; the inclusion of Poland in the EU will only facilitate their continued arrival and legal residence. Algerians, on the other hand, have encountered greater difficulties in obtaining visas for Italy; instead, they journey first to France, an easier task given their historic ties to their former colonial metropole, then cross the open border into Italy.[27]

As a general rule, foreigners present longest are most likely to enjoy legal status. The permit, so hard to obtain, is easy to lose and a chore to retain. As a long-resident Tunisian woman bitterly remarked, "We [immigrants] can't sleep at night for fear of losing this damn permit." The most recent immigration law (2002), which links the right to reside and work to proof of employment, has disturbed the sleep of many in Ragusa province. Owing to the short-term contracts prevalent in agriculture, even old greenhouse hands find themselves applying every year (if not more frequently) for this essential document. Immigrants and their advocates describe the immigration office in the Ragusa Questura (the provincial headquarters of the national police, or Polizia dello Stato) as excessively slow and bureaucratic, even by Italian standards. For the applicant, the process requires multiple trips to the city of Ragusa (about an hour by car from Santa Croce), lengthy waits, and the attendant loss of valuable income and the good will of employers. In early summer of 2004, many men found themselves stranded in Vittoria. Still waiting for their permits months after filing the application form, they were unable to make the summer journey back to Tunisia or Algeria. On account of extraordinarily low prices for tomatoes, farmers were hiring the absolute minimum number of hands. Many rose early each morning in a fruitless attempt to find work, then drifted through town, spending as little as possible of their precious savings.

The permit procedure turns even the longest-resident foreign worker into a ritual supplicant. An Algerian merchant in Santa Croce made the point forcefully. He discreetly nodded in the direction of one of his customers, a deeply tanned Tunisian well into his fifties. "He gave his youth to the greenhouses. He's been here some thirty years and does he get a *carta soggiorno* [the long-term permit, for which one is normally eligible after five years, and similar to the "green card" in the United States]? No!" To the speaker, this showed, on the part of the Sicilian authorities, a profound lack of respect for the man's contribution to the local economy and for the magnitude of his personal sacrifice.

The North African presence exemplifies the phenomenon of chain migration in which people move as the result of personal networks rather than active recruitment by employers and agencies. Virtually everyone has arrived in the area on the advice or with the help of a family member, neighbor, or friend. Sami, a semi-professional soccer player in Monastir, Tunisia, came in 2002 on the advice of a buddy. Tahar, also a compatriot, arrived in the mid-1990s; when his attempt to pursue graduate studies in France stalled, his uncles called him down to the greenhouses. Karim, a barber in Jejol, in northwest Algeria, followed a brother. Because chain movements are driven by personal connections, they tend to cultivate very specific pathways between places and populations. Most Tunisians in Vittoria, for example, share a handful of surnames, a clear indication of their shared origins. Of course, natives of the capital city of Tunis or other northern localities are found in Vittoria, but the vast majority hail from the rural areas near Kairouan and Madhia. Don Beniamino Sacco, whose Caritas program in Vittoria has hosted thousands of Tunisians over the past ten years, jokes that although he has never set foot in Tunisia he is one of the best-known men in Kairouan. Upon arrival in Vittoria, newcomers from that part of Tunisia always ask directions to Don Sacco's place.[28]

Observers describe these men as rural folk, old-fashioned peasants, accustomed to hard physical labor, conservative of outlook, and with scant classroom experience. Their hometowns are characterized by declining agriculture, low wages, high unemployment, and, in the context of two decades of remittances, increased living costs. As one immigrant observed, "Even if a young man got a job, he couldn't achieve a quarter of his ambitions in that place." As the migratory chain has developed, more men and women in Tunisia have gained knowledge about life in Sicily and have come to regard a sojourn there as a distinct possibility. Lack of opportunity clearly predisposes people to consider leaving, but it is the emergence of networks that makes the migratory project possible for so many. These men envision their migratory project as temporary: between six and ten years of hard labor will, they hope, result in enough money to build a house and possibly establish a modest business back home.

The migratory chain is forged and lengthened every day and every year. The telephone centers in Vittoria and Santa Croce do a thriving business as men call home to family and friends in Tunisia and Algeria. Remittances build additions, even whole houses, and furnish them in a manner befitting the elevated status of the occupants. On summer and winter visits home, immigrants describe life in Italy, boast of their achievements, and show off new acquisitions.[29] As embodiments of European wealth, consumer goods figure prominently in the immigrant experience.

Samia, a Tunisian woman who arrived in Sicily long after her father had come to work in the greenhouses, recalled how the early immigrants sought to transport back home "everything," from domestic appliances to toiletries to clothes. The automobiles of the proud men labored under mountains of goods; men tugged at ridiculously huge boxes full to bursting. She fondly remembers receiving a doll that walked, her first real toy and the envy of neighborhood kids. But the most memorable thing of all was the television. Samia and her companions normally played outside, happily inventing games. The thrilling event came at 4 p.m., when a Charlie Chaplin film was broadcast by the state television station, and dozens of children and adults would pile into her family's small home. Parents on the street sent letters of thanks for the wonderful device to her father in distant Vittoria.

Over time, the opening of larger stores and the establishment of factories in Tunisia have made redundant the shipment of many goods from Italy. Today returning immigrants favor suitcases stuffed with well-known brands of clothing to wear, sell, and give away. Typical is an Algerian man who described his favorite apparel—shoes by Puma, shirts by Nike, jeans by Levis.

In the last few years a new population has joined the Tunisian and Algerian men in the greenhouses. When we returned to the area in early summer of 2004 after an absence of just over a year, people were quick to point out the gathering presence of Polish women. Among North African men gathered in the piazzas and at telephone centers, a rumor circulated that Polish (and other Easterner European) couples were accepting combined daily wages as low as 20 Euros, or less than one-third of the contractual rate (the contract governing agricultural work is described later). Tunisian women in Santa Croce confided in Sicilian friends their fears that their husbands' incomes would be threatened at the same time that their interest would be aroused by proximity to such "beautiful" (that is, blond) co-workers. A Tunisian unionist predicted darkly that given the eastward expansion of the EU, these "ladies from the East" would soon replace North African men in the greenhouses.

On the basis of discussion with social workers, employers, and unionists and a visit to a farm with Polish workers, we offer the following sketch of an emerging phenomenon. The women first appeared on farms in 2001 or 2002. In contrast to the personal links drawing North African to the area, these women arrive by means of informal employment services, paying a fee to a countrywoman who places them with an employer. Typically a woman works for two or three months, until her tourist visa expires, then returns home with cash enough to invest in housing or some other big purchase. Once a group of women returns they are replaced by another in a rotating system. (Polish men sometimes work in greenhouses, too; they prefer to invest in cars, which they drive home for sale.) The women rarely leave the farms where they live for fear of detection by the authorities or for reasons of work. The dimensions of the influx are unknown, but a representative for the union CISL[30] estimated 200 to 300 Poles live in the Vittoria area.

The farmer we met reported that he started the women at 20 or 30 Euro per day, then raised pay to 30 or 35 in line with performance. Over the last two years he has replaced North African men with Polish women because they are better, not necessarily cheaper, workers. "One woman works as much as three men," he stated. And whereas the North African men talk of their "rights" and move slowly, the Polish women work productively from the very first hour. This farmer certainly felt more comfortable managing a white, female, Catholic workforce than a male, Muslim, North African one. He claimed that he treated the women well, occasionally taking them to the beach or out for pizza, and making sure that he or a Sicilian colleague performed the heaviest lifting. Other farmers however work the women mercilessly and, he hinted, request sexual favors. The Polish presence, for a series of reasons, represents an important change in the population of greenhouse laborers, albeit one with unknown future ramifications. At the same time, the women simply make up the latest in a series of foreigners whose compulsion to work hard for little (by Sicilian standards) keeps the system afloat.

WORK UNDER THE PLASTIC CEILING

The greenhouse system determines the activities of most foreigners in the Vittoria–Santa Croce area. Typically, cultivation begins in September and concludes in December. First, old plant material is removed, and the soil under the plastic sterilized. Young plants obtained from nearby nurseries are planted at regular intervals along strips of heavy plastic sheeting. With a regime of irrigation and spraying, the plants grow rapidly and begin producing in a matter of weeks. Harvesting soon begins in earnest, interspersed with periodic pruning, training, and spraying. From January to early June the process is repeated. For many years, in July and August, when extreme heat and the glut of open field production made greenhouse cultivation impractical, the plastic sheeting was removed, repairs effected, and the beds readied for the fall season. Many producers today stagger planting in order to produce year-round. In the hottest months, they remove or roll up the plastic ceiling. As work falls off toward early summer, many immigrants travel to western Sicily for the grape harvest or cross the Strait of Messina to the southern Italian mainland to toil in tomato fields. Like January, summer provides the opportunity for the all but obligatory trip home to Tunisia or Algeria.

In some respects, the introduction of new materials and techniques has eased the burden of greenhouse work. While the soil was formerly prepared by hand, wider doorways now permit mechanical cultivation. Drip hoses have replaced the tiny irrigation canals dug with the traditional short-handled hoe. Plastic roofing, which used to be nailed up and torn off each season, is now durable enough to last several seasons and is rolled up in the summer months. Crate capacity has shrunk from twenty to ten kilograms, making harvesting itself less arduous.

Still, greenhouse work remains dirty and demanding. These hardships are compounded by the nature of agriculture. The daily regime of bending, stretching, lifting, often in tight spaces, wearies the strongest man or woman. In describing why local youth refuse such employment, Mayor Aiello compared it to labor in the infamous sulfur mines of the past. For ten hours or more, six days a week, workers spray, weed, harvest, and harvest still more. Under the plastic ceiling, temperatures soar well above 100 degrees Fahrenheit (38 degrees Centigrade) by late spring. By summertime, work ceases in the greenhouses by midday and resumes later in the afternoon. Still, even at 4 p.m. the heat is formidable. "It's like working inside a giant plastic bag that's been left out in the sun," lamented a young Algerian. The casual gardener would not recognize these cherry tomato plants, which can reach over twenty-five feet in length; trained to climb up to a cable suspended below the ceiling and back to earth again, the plants form living partitions. Below, leaves are stripped to facilitate harvesting while under the roof they are left intact to protect the fruit from the searing sun. A Sicilian farmer aptly likened a greenhouse full of mature plants to "the jungle." Inside, one encounters a profusion of leaves, stems, and fruit, oppressive humidity and heat, and the distinctive acrid smell of the tomato plant.

Greenhouse work is also dangerous. Agriculture is a dangerous livelihood generally, and Ragusa ranks first nationally in terms of on-the-job accidents in the sector, according to union officials.[31] Workers commonly handle and inhale a variety of toxins designed to sterilize the soil, speed plant growth, and eliminate pests. Immigrants, who predominate among greenhouse workers and who often live on farms in close proximity to storage areas and greenhouses, suffer disproportionately.[32] They report regular physical discomfort and fearfully anticipate future consequences to exposure. Since 2003, Doctors without Borders has offered free medical care to immigrants in Vittoria. While posters advertise services in several languages, including Polish, the typical patient is a young North African male. Doctors attribute the joint and respiratory aliments common among the patients to the fact that many live on farms in structures lacking running water, heat, and electricity.[33]

EMPLOYERS AND EMPLOYEES

In theory, employer-employee relations are governed by the provincial contract for agricultural workers, an agreement signed by representatives of growers' associations and the three national unions (CGIL, CISL, and UIL).[34] As of spring 2003, the daily pay for a common laborer—most immigrants are so classified—is 38.20 Euro (then about US$46). By law the employer must also make a contribution in the worker's name amounting to nearly half of his salary to the national social security system. Workers employed for a minimum of fifty-one days for two consecutive years are eligible for an unemployment benefit, based on skill level and family status.[35] As long as their employment is documented and contributions made in their name, foreign workers may also enjoy these benefits.[36]

In reality, employer-employee relations usually depart from contractual norms, ranging from the mutually convenient to the highly exploitative. Most if not all agricultural enterprises underreport days worked, thereby saving on the hefty mandatory contributions. In 2003, about 40 percent of days worked in agriculture in Sicily were reported, according to CGIL officials.[37] Although it is in workers' interests to declare some of their days worked in order to become eligible for unemployment benefits, workers and growers often share an interest in avoiding taxes. Far more than Sicilians, immigrants experience exploitative labor relations. Those lacking authorization are particularly at risk. Fearing capture and deportation, they accept very long workdays and the worst tasks for low pay.[38] But all foreigners, including those with permits, can easily name a variety of employer abuses. "There are all kinds of bosses," observed Mounir, a Tunisian man with over a decade of experience, "but I'll bet that there's not a single one here who will give you all the law requires. Even the best will find a way to cut a corner." While acknowledging that Sicilian employees also suffered, he maintained that immigrants routinely endured the depredations of employers. Immigrants receive 30 or even 20 Euros for a day's work rather than the contractual rate. Farmers, aware of foreigners' need for proof of employment, may demand payment in exchange for a contract or, more commonly, extract concessions. In this way an extra quarter of an hour in the morning and evening becomes an hour, all without additional pay naturally. "And if you speak up, like I always do," continued Mounir,

> then they'll tell you to get the hell out, that they can replace you just like that. Threaten to report them and they call their boys to beat you. Oh, yeah, I've been beaten, a couple of times! They'll tell you that there's absolutely nothing you can do to them. And they're right, because no one, neither the Left nor the Right, protects us.

Housing is also a point of contention. Given the absence of housing in town and costs of travel, many North Africans reside on farms. While this is convenient and often costs little, proximity to the workplace can lead to abuses as some farmers feel free to assign their boarders tasks at any hour. Mounir observed that "some workers have houses at home far superior to their bosses' places, and the Sicilians don't even realize it. They treat you like an animal and then ask you to be grateful. This kind of disregard creates hate."

In a region where employers extend hospitality to Sicilian workers on special occasions, no such invitations are issued to immigrants. According to immigrants, farmers consider them strictly in monetary terms. According to the Algerian, Ali,

> You're just a tool, an animal to them. They won't let you out of the greenhouse even for a drink of water. When it suits them, they say we're all friends. Yes, on the farm the worker may eat with the farmer's family. But as soon as you're no longer working for them, they refuse to acknowledge you. I worked as a sharecropper for five years. Do you think that the guy says hello when we meet in town? No! It's incredible, these people are so ignorant!

Religious holidays are also indicative of the absence of social interaction. Union officials point with justifiable pride to the inclusion of contractual provisions recognizing the diversity of the workforce; Muslims, for example, may work half-days during Ramadan. But the reality of the agricultural workplace does not permit the observance of non-Christian holidays. Mounir explained how his compatriots practice Islam the way most Italians practice Catholicism, that is, only on special days. He complained that he has always been forced to work holy days such as the Eid Al-Fitr celebration at the close of Ramadan but that he loses pay when farms shut down for Christian celebrations. "We plead with them to let us work, but they throw up their arms and say 'you have to understand, we have family visiting.' This is really hard to hear when I'm missing both my pay and my family."

It is natural that an underpaid and overworked foreign workforce should dwell on the sins of Sicilians. But, as they admit, not all employers are cads, not all immigrants saints. On small farms, foreign workers commonly share the midday meal with the family. Accommodations on farms, while often crude, are usually free and can be equipped much better than apartments for rent in town. It is also worth stressing that the farmer needs to cultivate trust among his workers because the very survival of his business depends on the willing arms and legs of mobile foreign workers. When weighing the inevitable requests for contracts and assistance in regularizing status, employers consider each individual's performance and reliability. Many have devoted time and energy to the permit process with the understanding that the worker so aided will become a regular only to find the immigrant fails to return after the summer break. The casual attitude toward clock and calendar among North Africans has also disrupted work on more than one farm.

It is also worth noting that immigrant workers in Ragusa appear more likely to be documented and receive contractual pay than their peers elsewhere in Sicily.[39] In large measure this is the fruit of union activity. In Santa Croce and Vittoria, immigrants soon understood that CGIL and CISL in particular offered them helpful information and meaningful support. For the last two decades, union representatives have enrolled foreigners, filed paperwork on their behalf, spoken with employers, and negotiated with government authorities and with farmers' unions. They maintain that all workers are entitled to the protections and pay specified by national labor laws and the provincial contract. The value immigrants place in union membership is indicated by the numbers: in Vittoria, with a registered foreign population of 4,000, CGIL boasted about 1,300 members while CISL counted about 1,000 as of early summer of 2004. Stiffer employer sanctions and increased scrutiny by the social security administration, at least since the mid-1990s, have also cut down on the incidence of undocumented employment in the area.

In response to rising costs associated with reporting all (or most) employees, farmers have experimented with so-called *compartecipazione* agreements in which the farmer provides the greenhouse and materials, the immigrants provide labor, and the two share eventual profits. Hailed at the time (the 1990s) as a step on the road to immigrant entrepreneurial activity, the innovation satisfied neither population. Sicilian landowners complained of the unreliability of their Tunisian partners. To their dismay, the latter found that as entrepreneurs they no longer qualified for the benefits they enjoyed as workers and that the promised rewards for hard work seldom materialized after the costs of production were tallied. On the positive side, sharecropping exposed immigrants to farm management. In recent years, a few Tunisians and Algerians have begun to rent land outright, assuming all the risks and benefiting from the successes of production.

Consider the case of Ali, a burly Algerian who has adopted the mannerisms of the Sicilian peasant and favors piquant expressions of social commentary. He first learned of the possibilities of the area from a fellow merchant in northeast Algeria. After a reconnaissance mission, he decided to stake a claim to Vittoria's green gold. After several tense years living without a permit, he regularized his status under the 1995 amnesty. He performed day labor, then learned the business as a sharecropper until he had accumulated sufficient capital to rent land himself. Today, "just like all the other farmers," he owns the equipment, tools, and vehicles needed for cultivation. A typical small farmer, he performs all the labor himself, with an occasional hand from his wife. Like others, he quits by midday when the greenhouses become "like an oven," then returns in the evening. While the work is brutal, he can make a living and he is able to determine his own schedule.

Very few immigrants can afford to be their own masters, however. Local farmers reckon 4,000 square meters of greenhouse to be the minimum required to maintain a family. According to their calculations, the cost of cultivating a crop of cherry tomatoes in such a structure runs to about 12,000 Euros (US$14,400 in 2004). Even granting that an immigrant requires less disposable income than his Sicilian counterpart, few foreigners can amass this kind of cash. They are thus destined to remain laborers.

LIFE ON THE MARGINS

Local residents were taken aback by the sudden arrival of Tunisian men in the 1980s. Like the Sicilian peasants before them, immigrants would gather before dawn in designated local squares, hoping to meet an employer. Tunisian men assembled again in the evening and on Sundays, to socialize and share news from home. At night they slept wherever they could lay their heads. Some repaired to outbuildings on the farms where they worked while others took refuge under plastic sheeting in the fields. A few rented apartments while others occupied abandoned or unfinished buildings in towns. Few had access to running water, toilets, or showers, to the detriment of their own hygiene and the appearance of areas they frequented. They endured these deprivations as a temporary sacrifice that would permit them to save money to send home. Lonely, with cash in hand and far from the social support and restrictions of Tunisian society, some turned to drink. With no place to congregate other than the town square, their occasional bouts of drunkenness and loud disagreements presented disagreeable public spectacles.

The reactions of townsfolk varied from pity to disgust. Renting even the worst accommodations was difficult for the newcomers. In Santa Croce, landlords complained of finding a dozen men in apartments they had rented to just one or two. Some businesses refused to admit Tunisians, claiming that they disturbed respectable customers. In Vittoria, parents refused to bring their children to the city park, where many immigrants camped out. The homeless men relieved themselves where they could. The city installed temporary services for immigrants but withdrew them after residents complained of city monies benefiting foreigners. Episodes of immigrant misdeeds received much attention in the local media. In private, strong words condemned Tunisians as filthy brutes, a menace to public order. Objections took on a gendered dimension as well. Parents cautioned daughters to avoid areas frequented by Tunisians and urged them to have nothing to do with them.

Immigrants could not help but notice these attitudes. In a 1994 Caritas study, the Tunisian Gharbi Imed describes how the shock of understanding his pariah status was even more difficult than rising at 3:30 a.m. in search of hard labor:

> Instead, the thing that bothered me most at first, but which I see now has surely changed, was the reactions of Vittorese toward me. It was really hard for me to accept that a girl, or a youth, or an old person whom I met on the street would avoid me as if I had some terrible sickness. Or would steer clear of me for fear of being robbed, as if all the thieves and criminals were immigrants.[40]

Some local youth and activists did cross the line. As noted earlier, union representatives enrolled foreign workers, assisted with paperwork, and monitored employer-employee relations as best they could. In time they would hire immigrants as union employees to serve their foreign members better. They also helped fulfill immigrants' wishes for social spaces of their own; in both towns Tunisian and Algerian men's clubs were formed. Church representatives and volunteers also responded quickly. While Caritas (a worldwide charitable organization sponsored by the

Catholic Church) assists all in need regardless of nationality, most visitors were in fact Tunisian. In both areas, Caritas centers strove to address basic needs, serving up hot meals and offering dormitories and showers. Personnel gave out clothing, fielded calls from prospective employers, assisted with paperwork and other bureaucratic matters, and offered countless other services. Caritas representatives met with authorities and generally cultivated an understanding of the immigrant situation and Sicilian responsibility among the public. Both Bartolo Scillieri in Santa Croce and Don Beniamino Sacco in Vittoria describe local reactions as an amalgam of charity, ignorance, and hypocrisy. Outright hostility to Tunisians, they note, has all but disappeared in the last decade.

By the late 1990s, the sense of emergency and climate of fear had subsided, and the situation of immigrants had improved. Many carry permits and hold documented jobs. With pride they can recount how their families now live better thanks to their labor in Sicily. While their living conditions remain substandard, almost all foreigners now have a roof over their head. Longer-resident immigrants are donning better clothes, acquiring cars, even purchasing apartments. Greenhouse rental and entrepreneurial activity also indicate a measure of success and signal a long-term commitment to life in Sicily. In both Vittoria and Santa Croce, small numbers of Tunisian and Algeria men frequent storefront locales for Muslim prayers. Ubiquitous phone centers provide access to communications, shops offer sundry North African goods, and grocery stores sell immigrant foodstuffs, including *halal* meat prepared according to Islamic rules. A weekly bus service brings patrons to the ferry for Tunis. As we will see next, men who have secured a livelihood are most likely to form families in Sicily and invest in an Italian future.

Today, relations between Sicilians and Tunisians are cordial, if distant. Despite growing numbers of family reunifications, most immigrants are even today unaccompanied males who view their presence as temporary.[41] They endure hardships to amass funds to build a house, support a family, perhaps start a business. Their affective life and aspirations remain firmly rooted in family and locality in Tunisia and Algeria. With very few exceptions, immigrants harbor no desire to establish associations, pursue common goals, or interact socially with Sicilians. Social workers, priests, and others favoring integration describe North Africans as "closed" toward Italians and perhaps the West in general. Tunisian and Algerian cultural mediators, who have struggled to forge intercultural dialogue, complain that most North Africans prefer the comforts of family and co-villagers—which are found in abundance, thanks to chain migration—to the challenges of the wider world. Summarizing the limited worldview of the conservative peasant type prevalent among Tunisians, an experienced Tunisian mediator stated, "for

GIRARROSTO
SPECIALITA' ALLA BRACE

POLLO ALLO SPIEDO
CARNE ALLA BRACE
AGNELLO - CASTRATO
SALSICCIA MERGHES
GOLOSIE ARABI   Tel. 360 517264

Photo 4.4.   Immigrant food shop, Vittoria

them, the concept of the 'other' doesn't exist. They can think only of doing things one way—their way!"

Sicilians, for their part, have come to see Tunisians as an economic necessity and accept the idea of greater immigrant rights. The open animosity of the past has disappeared, replaced by apathy toward the immigrant
situation and suspicion regarding the merits of foreigners. Ali recalled
how people used to spit at him and shout obscenities. Such intimidation
proved useless, he observed, "for the Arab man knows no fear." Things
have improved dramatically and newcomers no longer have to suffer as
he once did. Appalled by the ignorance of Sicilians, he opined wryly, "in
another fifteen years maybe we can make them [the Vittorese] a modern
people! They say we're from the Third World, but they're, I don't know,
from the Fourth or Fifth!" Criticisms about the lack of modernity in Sicily
are not uncommon among immigrants who fail to find the efficient Europe of their imagination. Others fault Sicilians for failing to treat immigrants as equals. Another Algerian, a merchant, observed that because
they are treated without respect, some immigrants cut a bad figure. Some
do so because they have lost respect for themselves in Sicily while others
rebel at the belittling treatment they receive.

Sicilian advocates of immigrants note the indifference of Sicilians to the
suffering of their foreign neighbors as well as the prejudices they may harbor against them. Advocates also lament the lack of any sustained effort on
the part of political leaders. Cultural events and organized get-togethers

remain rare, the product of individual initiative. Only for some elements has the Church been able and willing to make a difference, to address immediate needs left unattended by government agencies. In Vittoria, the Caritas center at Santo Spirito continues to provide hot meals and beds to about 200 people daily. The Caritas program in Santa Croce has taken a different approach. Viewing the situation of immigrants as much improved and no longer an emergency, and cognizant of their limited resources, the leadership recently decided to quit offering *prima accoglienza* (basic services like showers and meals) in favor of longer-term goals. In 2002, Santa Croce joined Itaca Sud, a Caritas program dedicated to facilitating the integration of immigrant families in southern Italy. Volunteers aim to improve the situation of immigrant families by coordinating the responses of schools and local government offices.

Gender relations and religious differences continue to generate suspicion and misunderstandings. The unattached North African male is perceived as a danger to Sicilian women. Algerian and Tunisian men complain that when they approach, Sicilian women will cross the street as if to avoid a threat. Shopkeepers will hurriedly serve a North African man before other customers in order to be rid of this charged presence, and female customers will go out of their way to avoid walking past them in stores. Local women are made to understand that the Tunisian man, no matter how seemingly open as a suitor, will in marriage limit his wife's freedom and insist on the precedence of North African and Islamic custom. That the few mixed marriages in the town usually involve Sicilian women of low status and few options only reinforces the association of marriage with a Tunisian as a social disaster.

Anxiety and misunderstanding cuts the other way, too. Aberrahman, an Algerian businessman in Santa Croce and a trained professional at home, admitted that he, like so many fellow North Africans, assumed that European women were promiscuous. The prospect of rampant shamelessness appalled him, for as a good Muslim he had been taught to repress sexual urges and keep a respectful distance from unrelated women. After residing in Sicily for a time, however, Aberrahman grasped that while unrelated men and women did in fact interact more frequently than he deemed proper, they nevertheless obeyed a set of moral guidelines. Relations with Arab men and Sicilian women are quite rare. For the men, fear and desire mingle, resulting in appreciation at a distance. When brought into close contact with Sicilian women—for example at a union meeting—most men act reserved, awkward, and keep their distance.

Sicily, situated in the middle of the Mediterranean Sea, has long participated in the struggles and accommodations of the Christian and Muslim worlds. The millions of Muslims resident in Europe today are often portrayed as unable to assimilate to the West's Judeo-Christian and secular humanistic heritage if not actively hostile to it. Recent terrorist attacks in Europe and the United States, most notably the 2001 attacks in the United States, the 2004 bombing in Madrid, and the bombings in London a year later have solidified the image in the West of a violent and implacable Islam. There have been no attacks or clashes in Sicily, but Muslims feel under scrutiny by virtue of their faith alone.

In the Vittoria area, Muslims are keenly aware that Sicilians consider Islam itself suspect and that the Italian state actively monitors Muslim groups. The North Africans with whom we spoke feel misunderstood and unjustly accused of antisocial views. In 2004, Aberrahman, who sports a short beard, reported that he had recently been asked pointedly about his business in offices about town and had been greeted with shouts of "bin Laden" more than once. He complained that Sicilians fail to grasp the diversity of the Muslim world. "In Algeria, we have female doctors and engineers, women who drive cars and go to the beach. It's not like Saudi Arabia." Rather than explore the honorable tenets of his faith, his hosts reduce Islam to two exaggerations—the fanatic nurturing *jihad* against the West and the tyrannical husband who deprives his wife of liberty. Few of the thousands of North Africans in the Vittoria area could be described as devout, much less as fundamentalist, as is evident in the meager attendance at storefront places of worship. The devout are most likely to take umbrage at what they decry as the misleading portrayal of Islam in Western media. But in the post 9/11 atmosphere the majority cannot help but feel uncomfortable and under suspicion by virtue of their origins.

A MAN'S WORLD

The world of the North African immigrant in the Vittoria area remains a distinctly male one. At the end of 2002, for example, men made up almost 84 percent of the total of nearly 2,300 permit-holding adult Tunisians,[42] and the unregistered population surely boasts a higher percentage of males. The life of the unattached man revolves around work—securing it, performing it, getting paid for it, and remitting its gains. The typical Algerian or Tunisian rises early and works until about noon, when the greenhouses become unbearably hot. After a lunch break, he returns to labor, perhaps first packing the morning's harvest for the trip to the market before returning to the hothouse. After a long and arduous day, he has dinner, cleans up if possible, socializes if he has the energy and means, then goes to bed in anticipation for another day of toil. Those who live in town must find a way to the farm, driving or paying a small fee to a co-national car owner. Those living on the farm are spared the time and expense of the commute. But the rural setting offers few diversions, and those living on their employer's property can find themselves working longer hours than their urban peers.

The unlucky ones without steady employment rise early and make their way to the town squares where employers engage day laborers. If he fails to obtain work, a man spends much of the day outside in the company of other men. If he is lodging at the Caritas center in Vittoria, he is required to quit the place during the day; if he is sharing a cramped apartment with other immigrants, he probably prefers to get fresh air. A man with time to kill may stop at one of the squares where foreigners gather. He may drop in at a telephone center to chat, savor a cheap coffee, listen to music and news from home, perhaps place a call.

For most, leisure time is limited to Saturday evening and Sunday. Country dwellers catch a ride, even walk to town. Men gather in and around immigrant businesses, stroll about town, collect in squares. In Vittoria, there is a well-trodden path between Piazza del Popolo, the central square in which foreign and older Sicilian men form separate groups, and the immigrant-dominated Piazza Manin. Some frequent one of a handful of men's social clubs. Usually sharing origins in Tunisia or Algeria, habitués play cards, chat, drink coffee, and smoke. They are avid television viewers as well, favoring sports and news. In the middle of a discussion about what he had experienced living in Europe, a Tunisian remarked that freedom of communication had changed his views. He had learned more about his own part of the world by watching Al Jazeera, broadcast out of Qatar, than he had viewing the heavily censored Tunisian media.

North African men are, as a rule, very mobile. In part, this is simply a reflection of the seasonal demand for agricultural labor. As greenhouse production slackens, a man may move to work the grape harvest elsewhere in Sicily or across the Strait of Messina in southern Italy. The absence of affective ties to Sicilians and the view of immigration as temporary also prompts many to return home to Algeria or Tunisia, legal status and finances permitting. As we have remarked, these trips provide occasions for the display of acquired goods and knowledge, and can encourage others to undertake a venture in Europe. In recent years, small but increasing numbers of men are considering staying for longer periods in Italy. A listless economy in Tunisia and political turmoil in Algeria promise little security for those who would invest their hard-earned Euros. Tightened regulations on entry into Italy make returning home for good an expensive proposition; should a man give up his right to reside in Italy only to fail at home, he would lose a great deal indeed. For some, an Italian future involves going north to find factory work,[43] but most remain in the Vittoria area where the demand for agricultural work is nearly continuous.

FAMILIES DIVIDED, FAMILIES REUNITED

Like domestic employment, work in agriculture causes disruptions in family life. In Vittoria–Santa Croce, many unattached men are married but prefer to keep their wives and children home despite the high personal toll of separation. Financial considerations go a long way toward explaining low rates of family reunification. The stable employment and lease required by Italian law to effect reunification are difficult to come by. Regarding their stay as temporary, they are reluctant to transfer their families to Sicily with its higher cost of living. The proximity of North Africa also allows frequent visits home, even on a workingman's salary.[44] In this way some have lived separate from their wives and children for the better part of ten or twenty years, returning home for important events and summer vacations.[45]

Infrequent family reunification also grows from cultural roots, as a Tunisian man explained. When we met Mounir in 2003, he had lived in the area for nearly fifteen years. He was twenty-nine when he arrived in Sicily after a long stint in the army. Unusual among older Tunisians, he speaks very good Italian and readily converses with Sicilians. In a conversation in a men's club, he described his failed engagement to a local woman. Her family feared he would transport their grandchildren to Tunisia despite his assurances to the contrary. They also worried about the influence of Islam on the little ones. He proposed that she instruct the children in Christianity while he would teach them the tenets of Islam. In the end these differences drew them apart. Later, Mounir married a woman from his hometown in northern Tunisia. Describing separation from her as a "disaster," he was making arrangements for her to join him when we met.

Mounir's personal experience and work with one of the unions give him a vantage point onto the plight of his countrymen. While dim prospects at home have induced some to bring their families to Sicily, most still favor leaving them in Tunisia. "Finances and all that aside, I'll tell you honestly that we're scared of losing our identity," he said. His compatriots, he explained, favored traditional male-female relations in which the husband represents the family in public and earns money and the wife remains in the private realm, tending to house and family. While the Tunisian legal system may protect gender equality before the law in a manner uncommon in the Muslim world, the social context works to maintain effective separation of the sexes. According to Mounir, Tunisians fear that their wives, once in Italy, will demand Italian-style family relations. Alternatively, the Italian state might attempt to enter one's family life. He recounted the story, widely discussed in Vittoria, of a Tunisian man who whose wife, recently arrived in Italy, remained indoors. Her

Italian neighbors, ignorant of the good woman's adherence to a cultural code of modesty, assumed the husband locked her inside against her will. Eventually they called the police, who, to the embarrassment of the couple, conducted an investigation. For Mounir, the episode represented an injustice and an invasion of privacy. The story may or may not be true, but its retelling certainly resonates with deep-seated anxieties. Similarly, family reunification can be stymied by the fear that children raised in Sicily will forsake their Tunisian heritage in favor of the ways and morality of the Italians, a theme to which we return later.

For Mounir, the identity crisis of the Tunisian male also takes on a geo-political dimension in the sense that some see their potential loss of authority at home as the daily reflection of the humbling of the (male) Muslim world by the West. By way of example he outlined the consequences of investments in factories in his hometown by American and European capitalists. The enterprises were initially hailed as a boon to working people and a boost to the Tunisian economy. But instead of offering a living wage to unemployed men, the firms sought out cheaper female workers. In the six-month "training period" women earn even less although they could master the required skills in a week's time. Girls are now leaving school early to bring home a slim paycheck while grown men stand idle— a blow to the male right and duty to provide for his family.[46] Mounir's own brother, "as big as a door," is reduced to chauffeuring their sister and Mounir's wife to and from the factory. Because money brings power, women have begun to demand more say in family matters, even demanding that men take over some household chores traditionally performed by women. For Mounir, this debacle epitomizes Western hypocrisy. "You bring us all this in the name of freedom, but it overturns our way of life and makes us [men] insignificant." He recoiled from the prospect that soon Tunisian men might resemble Sicilian ones, unable to act without their wife's approval.

Notwithstanding these concerns, wives and children have begun to join husbands and fathers in recent years. Many have come to the realization that Tunisia offers neither them nor their children the probability of economic stability let alone advancement. Education and upbringing on Italian soil, it is hoped, will permit their children to escape life under the plastic ceiling. In Santa Croce, there were no North African families reunified in 1985 but ten in 1990, seventeen in 1995, and twenty-nine in 2000, for a total of fifty-one Tunisian and five Algerian families; 2002 saw the arrival of fifteen Albanian families. In Vittoria, family reunification permits were issued to 286 people in seventy families, almost all Tunisian, in 1998; another 294 people came with family visas the following year.[47] We do not have more recent figures for family reunification but the growing numbers of minors and women and the declining proportion of male Tunisians indicate a trend to family formation.[48]

Family formation takes many expressions. After stabilizing his position a man may return home to marry. Back in Vittoria, the newlyweds establish a residence and begin a family. In another common scenario, a married man tires of separation and calls for his wife and some or all of their children. Another, realizing the difficulties now involved in bringing over grown children, calls for a teenage son. Thus, families may include father and son, husband and wife, or the couple and some or all of their offspring (born at home or in Sicily).

IMMIGRANT FAMILY LIFE

However immigrant families may be constituted, life in Sicily spells change and challenge. For men, the presence of a family can exercise a moderating influence, making depression and recourse to drink much less likely. Notwithstanding the inevitable stresses of residence abroad, being with his family can give a husband a sense of accomplishment, a sense of being a complete person, not merely a disposable tool in the greenhouse system. After a long separation, simply joining the family around the dinner table can give immense satisfaction to parents and children alike. Others, overwhelmed by poverty and challenges to the patriarchal order, implode, giving occasion to bitterness and abuse. Every family navigates its own course, buoyed up and buffeted by the personalities involved, resources and liabilities, and the hand of fate. Virtually every interview and discussion, however, indicates that the often intertwined themes of parent-child relations, gender, and education constitute the points of greatest tension and change among immigrant families.

Gender relations vary in North Africa as in any complex society. It is safe to say that many Tunisian and Algerian men in the Vittoria area fear the deleterious effects of residence in Sicily upon their wives and daughters. Representative of the conservative male perspective is Mohammed, a young Algerian businessman in Vittoria. According to him, Algerian society is characterized by the notion of "respect," his term for a hierarchy based on age and gender. In this system, the son defers to the father and older brother, the wife to her husband, the girl to everyone. Thus a young man refrains from smoking or swearing or viewing a film with sexual content in the company of his father, and the woman lowers her voice in the presence of men. Because females are considered "weak"—undisciplined mentally and easily duped by a lustful man—they must be protected by men. According to this logic, allowing one's sister or wife out after 5 p.m. would signal that one's family does not care for her and that she is fair game for unrelated men found in public.[49] Considered from this angle, Sicilian society is shameless. Children speak back to parents; some may actually discuss birth control and sex with them. Unsupervised, mixed-sex groups of teenagers and young adults roam the streets well after darkness. The speaker acknowledged that some Sicilians do not permit such outrages, insisting instead upon an Arablike physical separation of the sexes, male guardianship of females within families, and complimentary gender roles. This pattern, observed Mohammed, had been the norm in the past, but sadly such commitment to strict morality is increasingly rare in Sicily today.

Some form of this male supremacy complex is widely diffused among North African immigrants in Vittoria. Husbands, considering themselves defenders of family virtue, feel honor-bound to demand modesty from wives and daughters. A man may insist on accompanying his wife to the market or Italian language courses. He may forbid the viewing of Italian television, with its scandalous female nudity and materialistic images. Installing a parabolic antenna, he will limit viewing to appropriate Arabic-language channels. He may discourage his wife or daughter from barring her shoulders or legs in the shameless manner of Sicilians.

Gender relations are strongly conditioned by the immigrant experience. A Tunisian unionist remarked that some of his friends who drank, smoked, and enjoyed nightlife at home have discovered their Muslim identity only in disco-rich Europe and have adopted a self-consciously pious stance. In a similar fashion a flexible, liberal view of women's possibilities held in Tunisia may turn rigidly conservative in Sicily. Such transformations are most pronounced among men, who feel most keenly the need to protect loved ones and display the ability to control something in a foreign land. A wife, particularly a young one without children, may find that in coming to modern Europe to meet the husband her family arranged for her, she has unwittingly exchanged the freedom to study and pursue a career for limitations reminiscent of her own mother's (or grandmother's) generation but without the support network that made that life rewarding. Women, too, can want to be seen as properly Tunisian or Algerian in Sicily, though to date this desire very rarely takes the form of veiling.[50]

With increased participation in and understanding of Italian society, the need (perceived on the part of men or women or both) to portray an explicitly North African identity through demeanor and attire may be felt less strongly or even challenged. With time, Tunisians have become more comfortable in Santa Croce. Tunisian wives interact with their Sicilian peers, especially neighbors, learning firsthand about the smaller families and more egalitarian gender relations of their hosts. Today most Tunisian women move about town, dress, and apply make-up as any Sicilian woman would do. As workers in packinghouses and less commonly in greenhouses, Tunisian women earn money, a capacity that can alter their status within the family. And taking Italian language courses brings them into contact with Sicilians as it enables them to communicate without reliance on their husbands. In 2004, ten Tunisian women were planning to start an association dedicated to the emancipation of female immigrants. Such an endeavor is bound to upset some Tunisian men and its success is uncertain, but such initiatives may point to way toward a future of greater opportunity for women.

With wives come children, and soon immigrant couples enter into more frequent and varied contact with Sicilians and their institutions. For parents, these encounters can be informative, frustrating, and pleasurable. They take pride in watching their children master a language that continues to bedevil them and hope that education will allow their offspring to achieve a good job far from the greenhouses. Yet they may bridle at the inversion of family power relations as their children assume the role of translator and guide. Parents, lamenting the laxity of their Italian counterparts, demand respectful behavior from their children, by force if necessary. Most will certainly make an effort to restrain daughters from circulating freely once they reach puberty. Parents also fear that in Sicily children will receive neither a proper grounding in Islam nor adequate training in Arabic—the two foundation stones of parental identity. For many, the perils of an Italian childhood outweigh the benefits, and they routinely send home children as young as six years of age to live with grandparents.

Others—and their numbers are growing—warily accept the challenges of childrearing in Sicily. North African parents anxiously watch their children adopt the foreign language and behaviors of their Sicilian age mates. School offers a powerful, multifaceted process for assimilation. In classrooms adorned with the crucifix, students learn a variety of subjects in Italian and are immersed in the Judeo-Christian and secular-humanistic traditions of the West. Pork may be served, Islam is a minority faith, and the nominally optional instruction in Catholicism is attended by virtually all Sicilian students. On the playground and around town, immigrant kids learn firsthand about the liberties afforded Sicilian youngsters of either sex. Yet parents realize that an Italian education may provide their children with the means to move far beyond the plastic ceiling.

It is true that even today only a minority of Tunisians (and other foreigners) are forming families and that even fewer still are entrusting their children to Italian schools. Yet the ranks of these pioneers are swelling, especially in the conducive environment of Santa Croce. According to Scillieri,[51] these families are cautiously putting down roots. Without stating outright their intention to stake a future in Italy, they are investing in businesses and housing in Sicily and not at home. Some have enrolled children in local schools, while others have grown children pursuing further studies or working in local shops. Some have begun to dream out loud, saying, "My son, he'll be a doctor." Back in Vittoria, Ali expressed this sentiment with his usual directness. Asked if his three-year-old son would grow up to work in the greenhouses, he shot back, "I'd kill him first!"

A STORY

Samia's story, albeit exceptional in many regards, touches all the high-tension wires feeding parent-child and gender relations in immigrant households. As a teenager she first set foot in Vittoria in the early 1990s. Alert and outgoing, she quickly learned the language and made friends among Sicilians. She struggled to secure a place in the peer group at school and coped with the sting of being called an "ugly black." When we met in 2004, she was pursuing a degree in foreign languages at the University of Catania. As an employee of a big northern firm, she routinely travels the length and breadth of country, interacting for the most part with Italians.

Samia described family life as a protracted struggle pitting her, her sister, and her mother against her father. At first they rebelled silently, sneaking food during Ramadan or watching frivolous Italian television shows. A series of battles ensued—over her first visit to an Italian friend's house, over the sleeveless shirt, over the purchase of a bathing suit and a trip to the beach. Her father responded to such challenges to his authority with stern reprimands, even blows. "He doesn't regret it at all. He's convinced he did what a good Muslim father should do," she commented. Despite these valiant efforts to inculcate Tunisian and Muslim ideals, the children defiantly pursued their own paths. Samia described how he nearly lost consciousness when her sister announced her intention to become an actress. The last barrier is for one of the girls to bring home an Italian fiancé. "If I were to do that, he'd shoot himself. You know that while a Muslim man may marry a non-Muslim woman, it's unacceptable the other way around."

Like many older immigrants, her father lives in the past. "He doesn't think that Tunisian women go to the beach, drive cars, wear sleeveless shirts. If he were to return home, he'd have a heart attack!" Unlike others, he cannot return to Tunisia. As a political exile, he is condemned forever to return only in memory to the land of his birth. While asylum "killed" and beat down her father, life in Sicily has spurred her mother to change and grow. As a part-time housekeeper she has met Sicilian housewives and learned about Italian domestic life. Although her Italian was not as proficient as her husband's, she has acquired a driver's license, goes to the beach, and dons European-style clothing.

Fellow Tunisians regard the father as something of a failure for his inability to rule his own household. Co-nationals also judge Samia herself as less than the ideal Tunisian daughter, though this condemnation she knows also springs from the jealousies common among immigrants. Over time, some have come to appreciate her utility and abilities. As a trained cultural mediator and fluent Italian speaker with wide-ranging connections, she can make things happen. She has worked in schools, organized events, and played a role in securing a locale for Islamic worship.

Samia recognizes the exploitation and discrimination that buffet Tunisians and other newcomers. For growers, the men are little more than beasts of burden. The Tunisian government takes an interest only in the remittances the country has come to depend on. Horrified at the squalor and isolation in which Tunisian men (and women) live on some farms, she organized Italian language courses so that they might communicate their needs and learn about basic hygiene, medical services, and Italian society. Progress, in many cases, has been slow. Most Tunisians are peasants who have known only hard labor and who honor the ways of their grandfathers. In Sicily they have done nothing to widen their narrow definition of the acceptable and desirable.

Echoing the criticisms voiced by Sicilians who work with immigrants, Samia described Tunisian men as having no interest whatsoever in change (apart from enjoying consumer goods) or the exchange of ideas. They resist the notion that a girl deserves the same freedoms as a boy or that a woman can achieve outside the home. She may have won the battle against her own father, but she has seen too many girls and young women denied opportunities and even abused in the name of tradition and religion. Although she feels like an anomaly, neither Italian nor Tunisian, she feels most comfortable with Italians and rarely socializes with Tunisians. Because of her job and studies, Samia rarely gets back to Vittoria. When at home, she avoids cafés frequented by co-nationals; she knows from experience that lewd comments and aggressive stares will greet her. She is outraged that anyone would question her integrity simply because she drives a car, has a job, and dresses and talks like an Italian woman. As she said when we first met, "I'm the exception that should make us question the rule."

AGRICULTURAL SUBSIDIES

As in the case of domestic workers in Palermo, the situation of immigrants in the Vittoria area is strongly conditioned by local contexts of reception. Many of the older generation of Tunisians are peasants, true, but most of the younger Algerians and Tunisians did not know the hoe until arriving in Vittoria. Men from North Africa move to Italy by virtue of networks composed of family, friends, and co-nationals; these same social pathways channel new arrivals into the agricultural jobs held by their peers. Given their precarious legal status, limited knowledge of Italian, and few contacts among Sicilians, the men stand almost no chance of gaining better employment conditions. In recent years economic forces have propelled the costs of greenhouse production upward while increased competition has driven prices down, resulting in stagnating or declining wages. Immigrants, lacking the supports enjoyed by Sicilians, accept this dirty work, and the more such employment is associated with a denigrated, overworked, and underpaid population the less attractive the sector becomes to Sicilian youth. The arrival of Eastern Europeans has complicated further the situation of North Africans. The superior dependability and docility, perceived or real, of Polish women may well promote increased arrivals from the East to the detriment of resident Algerians and Tunisians. The wholesale substitution of the greenhouse workforce is unlikely, however. North African men perform a variety of agricultural tasks throughout the year while the women rotate through the area for short periods of harvest work. Should Easterners settle in Sicily, as North Africans fear, they too would face higher costs of living, join unions, and demand their rights as workers. Nevertheless, the ongoing expansion of the EU may well bring still other foreign workers to the greenhouses of Vittoria, perhaps engendering the conditions for the development of an ethnic hierarchy similar to that found in the domestic sector of Palermo.

Despite two decades of vigorous immigration, North Africans in the Vittoria area make up a world apart. Tunisians and Algerians rarely interact with Sicilians outside the workplace or union office. Very few are involved in any form of association that would bring them in regular contact with Sicilians or fellow immigrants. The few who operate shops serve only immigrants. Intermarriages are extremely rare and viewed with disapproval by both Sicilians and immigrants. North Africans chafe at derogatory Sicilian views of Islam and the Arab world while Sicilians fault immigrants for failing to reach out to Italian values and customs. In sum, there exists a kind of social barrier that few on either side wish to talk about much less surmount. One gets the impression that only the farmers would notice if immigrants were to disappear tomorrow. In contrast, newcomers in Palermo form a much smaller proportion of the overall population but the immigrant presence is palpable, part of the city's vital force. Immigrant shops and restaurants serve Sicilians as well as other immigrants. Foreigners often number Sicilians and immigrants from other parts of the globe among their acquaintances. And while immigrants do not hesitate to voice criticisms of Sicilians, they come to appreciate the city and, once established in the north, speak wistfully of Palermo as their adopted home.

The character of labor demand in agriculture is one, perhaps the most important, reason for the tenor of immigrant life in the Vittoria area. For Tunisians and Algerians, the slackening of work in the summer months and proximity to North Africa allow for annual visits home as well as additional work sojourns elsewhere in Sicily and mainland Italy. Sicilian authorities long turned a blind eye to the seasonal presence of the Tunisian "tourists" so necessary to agriculture; in linking permits to employment in a context in which most contracts are short-term, new immigration law continues to promote significant mobility among foreign agricultural workers. Given the high costs and bureaucratic obstacles of establishing a family in Italy together with worries over the corrosive influence of Western culture, most Tunisians and Algerians have reconciled themselves to living apart from family. The pain of separation is doubtless keen, but in this respect these men have an advantage over the female career domestics described in the previous chapter. For women living on their own, domestic employment is at odds with family life. Employers reluctantly allow domestic staff vacations and at any rate home is distant and expensive to visit. Residing far from one's children, or foregoing childbearing, can undercut a woman's identity. North African men in Sicily, on the other hand, are fulfilling cultural expectations by journeying out into the wider world to support a family and may return at will to the company of wife and children.

There are signs that a long-term engagement with Italy is beginning to challenge the commuter or sojourner mentality among North African men. As we have seen, among the better-established immigrants there is a recent trend toward family formation. Childrearing in Italy will entail powerful challenges and offer difficult choices for these typically conservative Muslim parents. As Samia's story suggests, much conflict and change will involve gender relations. But family formation will also bring immigrants into closer contact with Sicilians and their institutions, and equip willing people on both sides with the tools and confidence to approach the wall separating them. Owing to its small size and ongoing initiatives in favor of immigrant families, pursued with vigor by school staff and Caritas volunteers and supported by growing numbers of parents, Santa Croce may host more satisfying interrelations than have heretofore been the norm in the area. As for the future, it is probable that, like Samia, immigrant youth will create a hybrid identity, one that offends and confounds their parents and challenges the monocultural vision supported by Tunisia, and to a lesser extent, Italy. It is harder to predict whether most will remain to enrich the social mosaic of the Vittoria area or follow the northward path of so many other immigrants and Sicilian youth. Much will hinge on the economic opportunities afforded the second generation. Will they like their fathers scrape by on a series of short-term seasonal contracts? Will they become farmers in their own right, renting or perhaps owing land? Will an Italian education and upbringing permit them access to white collar employment?

If the domestic workers reviewed in the previous chapter offer an un-recognized subsidy to Sicilian families, newcomers toiling in Vittoria's greenhouses enable Sicilian agriculturalists to reap rewards in an in-creasingly competitive global marketplace for fruits and vegetables. Despite large rural populations and ancient agricultural traditions, North African countries ceased to be self-sufficient in the 1970s.[52] Mo-roccans, Algerians, and Tunisians consume more and more grain from the United States and the European Union. Across North Africa, chronic water problems, a shift to fruit and vegetable production for ex-port, and government policies favoring urban consumers over than ru-ral producers have contributed to this decline in productivity. The EU has used its muscle to open North African markets to its goods, includ-ing heavily subsidized wheat, at the same time that it has effectively blocked the entry of North African fruits and vegetables into EU mar-kets that would pose a competitive threat to its own farmers. In a man-ner reminiscent of relations between the United States and Mexico,[53] these processes feed the veritable exodus from the North African coun-tryside and in so doing furnish European farmers with many willing and needed hands. By tolerating significant numbers of undocumented foreigners and benefiting from their low-wage and flexible labor, especially in agriculture, European states like Italy have nurtured the dependence of farmers and consumers alike on a vulnerable and semi-legal foreign population. In Tunisia and Algeria, communities and fam-ilies have borne the cost of raising young men who will serve as inter-changeable, disposable workers in the dirty work in foreign fields and greenhouses. Complaints about government subsidies given to growers now accompany any discussion of trade and agriculture. It is time that this other form of subsidy, the unacknowledged one made by so many families and communities, enters the debate.

NOTES

1. Studies and documents with a bearing on agriculture and immigration in Ra-gusa, Sicily, and Italy generally include: Agosta and Chironi 2000; Bellassai and Scillieri 2000; Caritas Diocesana Ragusa 1994; Cirivello 2001; INEA 1998, 1999; Micciché 1987, 1997, 2000; and Scillieri 2000.

2. Following the local usage, we will drop Camerina from the name of the town.

3. GEOPA 2002: 5. These figures, based as they are on declared laborers, blatantly underestimate the role of immigrants. For instance, at 1,058, the number of non-EU agricultural workers listed for Italy as a whole, fails to match the figure for foreign workers in Santa Croce alone!

4. In the spring of 2003, a series of database searches, inquiries with relevant institutions such as Food and Agriculture Organization (FAO), the EU, agricultural workers' and growers' unions, research institutes, and scholarly associations turned up surprisingly few studies of foreign farm workers in Europe. For instance, the massive, multilingual bureaucracy of the EU possesses no study on the subject, according to the division's librarian. The European Federation of Food, Agriculture, and Tourism Workers' Unions (EFFAT) likewise scarcely addresses the phenomenon. The subject receives little consideration in the comprehensive annual report produced by the International Centre for Advanced Mediterranean Agronomic Studies (e.g., CIHEAM 2000). There are practical reasons for the lack of information: foreign farm workers typically live dispersed in the countryside and move from job to job and return home with the seasons. Given high rates of unauthorized presence and undocumented employment, they and their employers prefer to maintain a low profile. Scholars of immigration often describe foreign farm workers as an example of labor market segmentation—see, for example, Ambrosini (2001); Fakiolas (2000); King (2000); Mingione and Quassoli (2000); Pugliese (1993)—but very few have produced detailed studies of the phenomenon. The exceptions we have located include: Hoggart and Mendoza (1999); Iori and Mottura (1989); and Pugliese (1991).

5. This trend is most pronounced in the United States, where as a result of aggressive use of subcontractors by farmers, unions represent a fraction of the agriculture workforce (Griffith and Kissam 1995; Rothenberg 1998).

6. This is explained in Hoggart and Mendoza 1999 and Jiménez-Díaz 2003.

7. A similar situation prevails in the United States, where despite a policy of rigorous and militarized border control, more than a million Mexicans annually cross the border into the United States. Rothenburg (1998) and Heyman (2002) describe how INS (Immigration and Naturalization Service) agents policing the border come to terms with the realization that their superiors want the appearance rather than the reality of a defended border.

8. INEA 1999: 57–59.

9. Caritas di Roma 2000: 241.

10. INEA 1999: 16.

11. INEA 1999: 143.

12. Because permits are allotted on the basis of unemployment rates, Sicily and other southern Italian regions with high rates receive virtually no permits.

13. According to the online databases of ISTAT (Istituto Centrale di Statistica), as of 2003, 21.90 out of 100 employed persons were employed in agriculture in Ragusa province, compared with just 8.32 for the region of Sicily and 4.88 for Italy as a whole. The employment rate of Ragusa province also indicates economic health: as of 2003, the province's rate was 41.41, compared with 33.96 for Sicily and 44.82 for Italy as a whole (ISTAT 2006).

14. Greenhouses cover about 5,500 hectares and account for about one quarter of Italy's greenhouse production. According to industry estimates, over 4,000 firms employ about 12,000 people (3A 2002: 8).

15. CGIL, Confederazione Generale Italiana del Lavoro (Italian General Confederation of Labor); CGIL has long been active in the area (see the following note).

16. Absentee landlords, typically titled and living in luxury in Palermo, long controlled vast tracts and exercised awesome control over the populace. The majority, denied respect and the benefits of education and sound nutrition, crowded into tiny dwellings together with their animals. These *braccianti* (day laborers) survived by working long hours for a pittance on nobles' estates and by cultivating their own miniscule parcels of land.

With the establishment of the Italian state in 1861 and the subsequent development of a party-based political system, peasants began to organize for economic justice, including access to land, some of which lay uncultivated. Represented by leftist parties and a fledgling union movement, the land-poor registered gains, especially in Vittoria. Landowners and their allies proved formidable opponents, however, and peasant demonstrations were crushed with violence, their activities monitored by police, their intentions maligned in the press. The repression, coming on top of grinding poverty, spurred further emigration to the Americas. The struggle for land and recognition rekindled in the ashes left by World War I, only to be smothered when the Fascists seized control and abolished independent political organizations. With the establishment of a parliamentary democracy after World War II, the peasants again pressed their claims. Representatives of the Communist Party (Partito Comunista Italiano, or PCI) and the Italian General Confederation of Labor (Confederazione Generale Italiana del Lavoro, or CGIL) in particular guided the occupation of abandoned land, organized demonstrations and strikes, and called for land reform and systematic provincial development.

Despite police violence and the legal ploys of landlords, by the 1950s more and more peasants were gaining access to land. Under the provisions of the 1950 regional law on agrarian reform, estates over 200 hectares were slated for expropriation and distribution. The *imponibile di manodopera*, a kind of tax that constrained owners to hire laborers on the basis of the size of their holdings, provided much-needed income to day laborers. Anxious about impending expropriation, angry at the imposed costs of the *imponibile*, and cognizant of the declining profitability of their (for the most part unimproved) estates, owners began to sell land, especially undesirable tracts in the hills and along the coast. Land was also available through rental or sharecropping agreements. In the latter arrangement, dubbed *compartecipazione* locally, owner and sharecropper split the costs of seed, fertilizer, and pesticides; the owner assumes responsibility for the greenhouse, machinery, fuel, and water; and the parties split eventual profits. In 1960, CGIL and the PCI were able to formalize this arrangement and obtain unemployment insurance and health and others benefits for sharecroppers. This description draws on a conversation with Giuseppe Micciché in 2004 and on his work (Micciché 1987, 1997, and 2000).

17. Aiello 1987.

18. In contrast, government intervention has spurred greenhouse cultivation in parts of southern Spain (Jiménez-Díaz 2003).

19. The party is known as the Democrazia Cristiana, or DC.

20. The PCI, or Partito Comunista Italiano (Italian Communist Party), and the PSI, or Partito Socialista Italiano (Italian Socialist Party), respectively.

21. Personal communication, Bartolo Scillieri, June 2003.

22. Personal communication, Giovanni Formica, April 17, 2003.

23. The quotation comes from Giuseppe Giannetti, "Strangolati dalla Bossi-Fini, *Il Manifesto*, September 25, 2002.

24. Permits issued in the province over the past decade number: 3,248 (1994), 6,407 (1996), 10,642 (1999), 6,532 (2000), and 5,844 (2001) (Caritas di Roma 2001: 424; Caritas di Roma 2002: 431). The spike in 1999 is attributable to the 1998 amnesty program, which induced many undocumented people to regularize their status. The subsequent fall reflects several factors, including a movement to the industrial north of Italy, the saturation of the local labor market, and renewed crisis in agriculture. Recently, the numbers of foreigners have again risen, with local union officials predicting about 12,000 permits for 2003. As the volatility of official figures suggest, permits issued offer only a rough gauge of the immigrant presence.

25. According to the online databases of ISTAT (Istituto Centrale di Statistica), as of 2003, there were 27.95 resident foreigners per 1,000 inhabitants in Ragusa province, compared to 12.57 in Sicily and 34.38 in Italy (ISTAT 2006). If the sizable unauthorized foreign population of Ragusa province were included in this calculation, the rate would increase. Based on the estimates of the total number of foreigners resident in Vittoria (5,000) and Santa Croce (1,500), for instance, the actual rate is probably closer to 91 and 167, respectively.

26. In Vittoria, for example, the number of legally resident Tunisians jumped to 1,712 from 1,264 in 1995–1996 while the number of Algerians rose to 194 from just 3 in the same period.

27. At present (2006) more than a dozen Western European countries have open borders under the Schengen agreement.

28. Personal communication, April 2003. Some of the essays in Sacco (2002) describe encounters with immigrants.

29. Holmes-Eber (2003: 75–77) describes how immigrants in Europe often come home to Tunisia to join family for major celebrations and the summer vacation.

30. CISL, Confederazione Italiana Sindacati Lavoratori (Italian Confederation of Workers' Trade Unions).

31. This according to Giavatto (2001).

32. Action taken by the chemical producer DuPont in spring of 2002 points to the reality of occupational hazards. In response to numerous "intoxication incidents" in Ragusa greenhouses arising from the incorrect use of the corporation's products, DuPont worked with provincial health authorities to train about 250 North African workers. It also commissioned posters in Arabic and Italian describing correct practice. But such action is rare, and the long-term effects inconsequential. Because inspections by Italian health and labor authorities are virtually non-existent, safety issues receive little attention in the local community. This episode is reported on the corporation's website (www.dupont.com).

33. This was reported in *La Sicilia*, 25 May 2004.

34. Unione Italiana del Lavoro (Italian Labor Union) plays a lesser role in Vittoria and Santa Croce than do CGIL and CISL. The text describes the contract in

force January 2000 to December 2003; it has since been extended. The current contract establishes a pay scale below the national standard. Union officials, aware that such concessions have come under criticism, explain that pay reductions were the only means to retain jobs in the wake of the local crisis of the late 1990s. A CISL representative pointed out that the number of registered workers in Vittoria rose from about 3,000 in 1996 to almost 7,500 in 2001, indicating that the slight reduction in pay had bolstered employment (Personal communication, Salvatore Bocchieri, April 2003).

35. According to CGIL's 2004 "Guide to Unemployment in the Agricultural Field," unemployment benefits correspond to 30 percent of the salary for up to 180 days. The pamphlet explains in detail the complexities of benefits in the agricultural sector. This benefit, the product of pension system reform legislation, is offered to agricultural workers in most southern Italian provinces. Union spokesmen, who handle requests for these benefits, deem the system less than ideal and call it a sop to the southern power base of the Christian Democratic Party that long dominated national and Sicilian politics. They openly acknowledge that the monies are needed for working families to make ends meet. Benefits have also financed not a few greenhouse projects for landowners posing as laborers.

36. Of the 2,200 applications processed in 2003 by the Vittoria CISL office, for example, about 800 were submitted by immigrants (personal communication, Salvatore Bocchieri, April 2003).

37. Personal communication, Salvatore LoBalbo, June 2003.

38. In spring of 2003, union and municipal officials estimated that the number of undocumented foreigners in Vittoria alone ranged from 1,000 to 2,000. Of course, their numbers can vary widely from year to year, owing to the volume of new arrivals, labor market conditions, enforcement, and ever-changing Italian immigration law. In 2002, undocumented immigrant laborers in Ragusa settled for about half the going day rate, according to press reports (Giuseppe Giannetti, "Una Vittoria alla ricerca di immigrati," *Il Manifesto*, September 27, 2002).

39. This according to studies conducted by the Palermo office of INEA (see Agosta and Chironi 2000; Cirivello 2001).

40. Caritas Diocesana Ragusa 1994: 35.

41. According to the online databases of ISTAT (Istituto Centrale di Statistica), as of 2001, only 20.80 permits of stay for family reasons were issued per 100 permits in Ragusa province, compared to 34.15 for Sicily and 29.12 for Italy as a whole (ISTAT 2006).

42. These figures are for the city of Vittoria.

43. It is said that younger immigrants are most likely to go north in search of factory work. Daly (2001) reports on the northward movement of younger Tunisian men formerly resident in Mazara del Vallo in southwestern Sicily.

44. The cost of a one-way passage in the summer season cost about US$100 in 2005.

45. Holmes-Eber (2003: 98–99) notes that working adults in Tunisia are expected to share resources widely among immediate family, wider kin, and even close neighbors. This means that immigrant men in Sicily are in all probability supporting a number of individuals with their remittances.

46. In her account of Tunisian family life, Holmes-Eber (2003: 23) states: "Employment of women outside the home after marriage—particularly in low-status jobs such as maids, factory laborers or hotel workers—is considered shameful, a sign that the husband cannot provide adequately for his wife and family or afford to seclude his women."

47. Personal communication, Bartolo Scillieri, June 2003; Scillieri (2000: vii).

48. As the figures in note 39 indicate, the rate of family reunification in Ragusa province still lags far behind other areas in Sicily.

49. Holmes-Eber (2003) describes male and female space in Tunis in much the same terms.

50. According to Bartolo Scillieri (personal communication, June 2006), this has begun to happen in the aftermath of the U.S.-led invasion of Iraq.

51. Personal communication, Bartolo Scillieri, June 2003.

52. This is described by Collinson (1996) and White (1999).

53. Griffith and Kissam (1995) and Rothenburg (1998) describe these changes.

5

~~~

Trading in People, Selling Sex

In this third and final example of dirty work, we return to Palermo and the dangerous participation of Nigerian women in street prostitution. Several contexts of reception conspire to create a tragic situation for many Nigerians. As foreign nationals selling sex in Italy, they are engaged at best in a semilegal pursuit that brings them into frequent contact with Italian criminals and police. As black street prostitutes, the women find themselves at the bottom of a prestige and pay hierarchy in the most perilous segment of the commercial sex industry. Also setting these women apart is their status as trafficked persons. Virtually all Nigerian prostitutes in Palermo are or once were beholden to loosely structured, co-national criminal gangs. The same networks that permit the movement of women to Italy facilitate their long-term exploitation by means of intimidation, violence, and debt peonage. So powerful are the ties binding the women to traffickers that they rarely take advantage of programs provided for victims of trafficking until they have fulfilled their obligations to their exploiters. Although many exhibit remarkable resiliency, years of psychological and physical trauma and lack of legitimate employment history do not bode well for their integration into Italian society.

Nigerian prostitutes make up but a small fraction of immigrant Palermo, but they are hard to miss. Since their arrival in the early 1990s, Nigerians have greatly expanded the city's commercial sex scene, visibly soliciting customers day and night in parts of the old city and in nearby Favorita Park. Analysis of their plight points to the recent confluence of trafficking and the burgeoning commercial sex industry, and illustrates the promises and limitations of recent anti-trafficking measures adopted by the Italian government. Like the domestic and agricultural sectors previously examined, street prostitution has its own local history, rules and practices, ethnic and racial stereotypes, and characteristic patterns of immigrant mobility and integration. Conducting research on farm laborers and maids who may reside with their employers and who often lack permits poses formidable challenges, but these difficulties pale in comparison to those confronting ethnographers aspiring to investigate trafficking and street prostitution. The description that follows is therefore tentative, based on insights procured over several years from a variety of perspectives. We elected to forego attempting to contact active prostitutes, for several reasons. The criminals who control the trade and monitor the women are best avoided; trafficked women have good reason to conceal parts of their stories; finally, respectful of the hard-won trust social workers had cultivated with the women, we did not ask to join them on their nightly rounds. We did speak with a handful of former prostitutes. At times they were forthcoming, at others hesitant to go beyond generalities.[1] The descriptions offered here rely heavily on conversations with those whose work brings them into close contact with prostitutes and trafficking issues. These include immigrants and Sicilians working on street teams, legal consultants, representatives of cultural associations, and investigators for the two main national police forces, the Carabinieri and the Polizia.

TRADING IN PEOPLE

Over the past ten years international governmental organizations (IGOs), national governments and regional coalitions, and non-governmental organizations (NGOs) have become increasingly concerned with identifying and combating the trade in people. The International Organization for Migration (IOM), whose 1994 seminar did much to kindle interest in the subject, regularly issues reports on trafficking and has been active in anti-trafficking initiatives, particularly in Europe. At the 2000 United Nations Convention against Transnational Organized Crime, hosted in Palermo, participants drew up anti-trafficking protocols that were adopted by the general assembly the following year. The United Nations Office of the High Commissioner for Human Rights (OHCHR) has issued reports, developed guidelines for combating trafficking, and collaborated with a variety of organizations, including IOM, the Organization for Security and Co-operation in Europe (OSCE), and others. In 2002, the Council of the European Union adopted framework for anti-trafficking measures within the European Union; a number of EU member states, notably Italy, have implemented anti-trafficking programs.[2]

These diverse entities share a view of the phenomenon as a worrisome manifestation of international criminality and as a human rights abuse of the first order. According to the standard definition,[3] trafficking involves the recruitment, transportation, and long-term exploitation of a person's body or labor through the use of deception, coercion, violence and intimidation, and debt bondage. (In contrast, smuggling refers to the exchange of money for assistance in making an illegal border crossing.) While men, women, and children are forced to perform labor of all kinds, most attention has been focused on understanding and combating the sexual exploitation of women and girls (defined as females under the age of eighteen). High estimates run to 700,000 women and girls trafficked annually across the globe, with up to 120,000 arriving in Western Europe alone.[4] Despite a shared concern with trafficking for purposes of sexual exploitation, IGOs, NGOs, and governments do not always agree on the dimensions of the phenomenon. Nor do they necessarily share anti-trafficking strategies. IGOs and NGOs have criticized governments for turning a blind eye to trafficking and for deporting foreign sex workers for breaches of immigration or prostitution law rather than pursuing traffickers.[5]

According to police investigations and other reports, trafficking in Europe typically involves individuals and groups from the Balkans, countries of the former Soviet Union, and the focus of this account, Nigeria.[6] Exploiting corruption and poverty at home and possessing a firm understanding of illicit markets, Nigerian gangs have exported tens of thousands of young women to the booming sex markets of Western Europe since the late 1980s. Nigerian traffickers form a far-flung, horizontal network of individuals and small groups collaborating to recruit, transport, and sexually exploit women.[7] In the face of increased police scrutiny and competition from larger and vertically organized crime syndicates from Albanian and the former Soviet Union, the Nigerian system has proven remarkably resilient. The traffickers have adapted quickly to new constraints and opportunities even as they maintain the control over women so crucial to continued profitability. Like all traffickers, Nigerians make free use of intimidation, violence, and debt peonage; the Nigerian system stands out from others by virtue of the central role of female exploiters and the threat of supernatural sanction. We explore the workings of the Nigerian system of trafficking later, but first we consider the national and local contexts in which the women find themselves.

PROSTITUTION IN ITALY

Once in Italy, the conditions, constraints, and opportunities of the women are conditioned by a series of factors, including the organization of the commercial sex industry, the legal status of prostitution, immigration law, and the response of the Italian state. Italy's stature as one of Europe's largest sex markets owes much to newcomers. From the late 1980s, Italian roadsides and city streets have hosted a veritable parade of foreign women for hire. With the exception of a few police actions designed to embarrass clients by sending tickets to home addresses, Italian men purchased commercial sex with impunity for much of the 1990s. Apart from small numbers of transsexuals and transvestites, genetic women make up the overwhelming majority of the sector's workforce. Seasonal fluctuations, mobility, the absence of any registration system, the illicit nature of much sex work, and a notable if variable criminal presence render any tabulation approximate. Estimates of foreign prostitutes in Italy for the late 1990s range from 15,000 to about 25,000.[8] The largest populations include Nigerians, who account for over half of all foreign prostitutes, Albanians, Eastern Europeans, and Latin Americans. Like their Italian peers, foreign sex workers cluster in urban areas, near military bases, along trucking routes, and in tourist enclaves. Observers agree that foreigners make up at least half the total prostitute population and most of the sector's full-time workers.

By all accounts prostitutes, especially foreigners, are in great demand. According to a recent survey, nearly 9 percent of Italian men reported using a prostitute, with higher rates clustered in the north, in major urban areas, among older men, and among the well-educated.[9] Commercial sex offers men instant gratification and a respite from what are euphemistically called the "complexities" of modern gender relations. Said a university student of his frequent visits to prostitutes, "There are no complications, there's no discussion, no waste of time . . ."[10] Italian men prefer foreign prostitutes because they are younger than Italian career prostitutes, charge much less, and consent to unprotected sex. The women's poor Italian skills and desperation to earn money also grant clients greater leverage in the encounter. Replacing the Italian prostitute—the local outsider—foreign sex workers have become "object[s] at once exotic, new and interchangeable."[11] The sheer diversity, volume, and mobility of foreign prostitutes reinforce a view of them as saleable objects attractive to male consumers for their novelty and willingness to satisfy.

As is the case in much of Western Europe, commercial sex in Italy assumes many forms and entails a range of living and working conditions, autonomy, and level of risk, with foreigners occupying the lowest levels.[12] And here as elsewhere, foreign women in particular confront danger. Some, like the Nigerians described in this account, are beholden to their exploiters. Those who have entered the trade on their own or with a man friend, or those who have paid off their traffickers, enjoy a greater measure of control over their working and living conditions even if they pay a workplace fee to local thugs. Clients may beat, rob, and rape sex workers, and police may harass or arrest them and request sexual favors. Many street prostitutes engage in substance abuse (excluding for the most part intravenous use) and some agree to unprotected sex, for which they receive double or even triple the usual fee.

The legal status of foreign sex workers is complicated. The 1958 "Merlin Law" abolished state-regulated brothels and eliminated the mandatory registration system. As Mary Gibson[13] has shown, the current law permits the private practice of prostitution but forbids solicitation and prostitution in public places; it also criminalizes any person who incites, facilitates, or profits from the prostitution of another. While the activity is not illegal, neither is it legally recognized. Although this may appear a technicality, it leaves prostitutes without workplace protections and denies them the possibility of contributing toward the national pension plan. Because soliciting is illegal, police may, at their discretion, level "administrative" sanctions against sex workers. The inclusive definition of aiding and abetting a prostitute essentially criminalizes any relationship with a prostitute, from renting or sharing an apartment to fetching a packet of condoms. In this way the law severely constrains a prostitute's ability to enjoy anything approaching normal social relations.[14] Foreign sex workers face additional problems related to immigration law. While prostituting oneself is not a crime, being present on Italian soil without a valid permit is. From the mid-1990s, hundreds of Nigerian and other foreign street prostitutes have been deported annually on this basis. On the other hand, foreigners who possess valid permits may not be deported for prostitution as long as they are employed in another capacity, most commonly as "entertainers" in possession of short-term visas.

The foreign women who have transformed commercial sex into a public spectacle in Italy have become the objects of intense scrutiny and much debate in Italy. The public simultaneously pities them as abused innocents, despises them as common whores and a public nuisance, fears them as carriers of disease (especially the HIV virus), and regards their presence as a disturbing symptom of the condition of the contemporary Italian male. Media accounts carry photographs of scantily clad Albanians and Nigerians soliciting clients, peddling the stereotype of the exotic, erotic woman. Sensationalistic depictions of women held in captivity and forced onto the street by criminal gangs have fired the public imagination, and sparked debate and legislation.[15] Right-wing political parties have not hesitated to link immigrants, particularly sex workers, to the dangers of criminality, disease, and disorder. The Northern League, for example, has repeatedly proposed revising the current law on prostitution and establishing state-regulated brothels as a way to collect needed tax revenue, prevent exploitation, and eradicate foreign criminal groups. Under the

Center-Left government of the mid- to late 1990s, on the other hand, immigration law and modifications to the anti-slavery law facilitated the prosecution of trafficking for the purposes of sexual exploitation and afforded protections to victims. Meanwhile, scholars and activists have noted the complex organization of prostitution, and described the range of risks, rewards, and autonomy experienced by sex workers, including trafficked ones. They point out that trafficked women account for under 10 percent of all foreign prostitutes in Italy, though the percentage runs higher for some groups, notably Albanians and Nigerians.[16] The Committee for the Civil Rights of Prostitutes and other associations have fought for the recognition of prostitutes as full citizens and as workers even as they have alerted authorities to the brutal realties of trafficking.[17] From Turin to Rome to Palermo, NGOs and church and lay organizations offer health education, medical aid, legal assistance, shelter, and protection to immigrant sex workers.[18] Viewing these women as subject to, rather than the source of, danger and risk, they attempt to reduce sex workers' vulnerability to STDs, violence, exploitation, and deportation.

For the Nigerian women examined in this account, a key feature of the current Italian system is its anti-trafficking measures, which have been judged among the most progressive in Europe.[19] Under the provisions of Section 18 of the 1998 immigration law, victims of trafficking qualify for a series of supports and services. Once they enroll in a program, they are eligible for a renewable short-term residency permit, enter a rehabilitation program, and may later register with the state employment agency. Section 18 provides two avenues to legal status. In the judicial path, a woman collaborates with the authorities, providing evidence and testimony against her exploiters; she qualifies for police protection in a manner similar to those who turn state's evidence against the mafia. Most women, fearing reprisals, pursue a second path of social protection, electing simply to declare themselves victims, renounce the activity of prostitution, and enter programs run by accredited local associations funded by national and local government. From 1999, when the program became active until 2002, about 3,000 former sex workers, including some 1,300 Nigerians alone, had enrolled in Section 18 programs, with the vast majority opting for the social path.[20] The Ministry of Equal Opportunity has also raised public awareness of trafficking; established in 2000, the hotline it sponsors is serviced by dozens of social protection projects, including one in Palermo.

NIGERIANS TRANSFORM PROSTITUTION IN PALERMO

The arrival of Nigerians transformed the commercial sex market in the Sicilian capital. As recently as the late 1980s clients met with a limited selection of partners for purchase. A clutch of small, informal brothels had grown up with the dismantling of the state-regulated ones in the wake of the Merlin Law. In the seedier parts of the old city, a man could engage a member of the small corps of aging career sex workers who worked on the streets or in apartments maintained for encounters. As professionals, Sicilian prostitutes retained control over the encounter—insisting on condom use, for example—and charged accordingly. Transient native drug addicts, though they were younger and willing to perform for less, were considered undesirable because they could carry the HIV virus or other STDs as a result of needle sharing and unprotected sex.

In the mid-1980s, North Africans arrived, followed by Albanians and then Nigerians in the early 1990s. The Nigerians quickly dominated the street trade and their numbers grew rapidly. From the late 1990s up through the present (2006), Nigerians have been synonymous with the street trade, save the very occasional Italian, Albanian, or Tunisian woman and the Italian transsexual. Indoors, the situation is reversed with Columbians, Italians, and some Easterners rotating through small luxury brothels or working as call girls advertising through local newspapers.

Enumerating Nigerian prostitutes in Palermo is an exercise in estimation. The women are transient, moving from city to city, and as they typically lack permits they do not figure in official statistics. Furthermore, their numbers vary in response to demand and police action. It is safe to say that by 1998–1999 the situation was getting out of hand. Streets of the old city and the Favorita Park teemed with Nigerian women, and clients purchased sex quite publicly. The City Council considered adopting antiprostitution measures developed in the north; a ticket for illegal parking in Favorita Park could mean only one thing, and it was hoped that sending such summons to clients' home addresses would discourage the trade. The two major police forces, the Carabinieri (part of the Ministry of Defense) and the Polizia dello Stato (part of the Ministry of the Interior) made sweeps, conducted investigations, and made arrests. Since the 2001 establishment of an office dedicated to foreign criminality and prostitution, the Polizia have continued to monitor the trade and forced traffickers to change tactics.[21] In short, the Nigerian population increased in the city until the late 1990s, then declined to under 100 women as the police began in earnest the periodic sweeps and investigations that continue today.[22]

While the exact number of Nigerians is unclear, their clear numerical superiority on the street is indisputable. Their popularity among clients is surely a function of price and availability. Nigerians consistently offer themselves at prices well below those charged by others; in 2004 Nigerians charged about 20 to 25 Euros per encounter, Italians 50, and transsexuals 100. Recent arrivals from Nigeria are also more likely to accede to clients' demands for unprotected sex. Racial stereotypes too figure in the popularity of the Nigerians as Sicilian customers hanker after the supposedly "hot" African woman. Commenting on the popularity of Nigerian prostitutes in Palermo, a journalist identified the appeal of the Other as well as the sense of power a white man enjoys while possessing a woman of color.[23]

On closer inspection, the preeminence of the Nigerians in street prostitution may be the product of disadvantage. With very few exceptions, Nigerian women work the street, by far the most dangerous and worse-paying niche of the sex industry. Lighter skinned women in Palermo are rarely found on the street, instead clustering in brothels and working as call girls. As elsewhere in Italy, there obtains in commercial sex a kind of racial hierarchy not unlike that found in the domestic labor market. Also at issue is the balance of power between criminal organizations. In the last decade, Nigerian street prostitutes have been pushed to peripheral areas by competing foreign criminal groups operating across the Italian center and north. In this light the strong Nigerian presence in Palermo may simply reflect the relative poverty of the local market.[24]

On the other hand, the Nigerian presence in Palermo may indicate a special accommodation forged between the African gangs and the mafia, Sicilian organized crime. As self-styled "men of honor," mafiosi have traditionally refused to participate in activities, such as prostitution, deemed detrimental to the fair sex. One police investigator, comparing Palermo's modest sex market to the robust trade of the north, speculated that lack of demand in the Sicilian capital may be the result of the mafia's disinclination to condone prostitution. Police observe that individual Sicilians involve themselves with the Nigerians, for example by overcharging them for run-down apartments and otherwise aiding the trade, but they have yet to find evidence of any collaboration or agreement between the local and foreign criminals. Yet, most observers cannot imagine that the crime families who systematically and cruelly prey upon their own people would permit foreign entrepreneurs to conduct a lucrative business, even in prostitution, without exacting a fee. And, citing the well-known atrocities committed against women and children in the course of recent mafia wars, they dismiss the idea that mafiosi remain bound by traditional rules of engagement.

ON THE STREETS

According to social workers and police in Palermo and published accounts,[25] once a woman enters into a pact with traffickers, she is handed over to Nigerian male criminals. These "trolleys" furnish a small group of recruits with purchased or forged documents and transport[26] them to Europe, where they deliver them for a reported US\$12,000 to 14,000 each to the co-national madams who have commissioned the shipment. These "madams," themselves former prostitutes, take their charge's passport, establish the debt owed (typically US\$40,000 to 50,000), and inform her that prostitution is the means by which she will honor her debt. The madam uses the woman's earnings to pay expenses, takes a share for herself, and allots a portion to the woman. She remits much of the money to Nigeria though the exact division of spoils remains a mystery.

According to social workers and former prostitutes, virtually every facet of the trafficked woman's life is dictated by the madam and her associates. The madam outfits the novice, instructs her in the basics of the business, and introduces her to the group of women with whom she will work and live. Fearful or recalcitrant recruits are cajoled, threatened with violence and supernatural harm, and beaten. In addition to the now enormous debt, the woman must pay dearly for lodging, sundry expenses, the "joint" or place of work on the sidewalk, and whatever fines the madam chooses to levy for bad behavior. The madam selects the workplace in the city itself, and periodically sends one or two women to provincial centers. Drawing on a loose network of colleagues, the madam moves women from city to city every month or so. This gives clients the variety they crave, keeps the women from growing familiar with their surroundings, impedes police investigation, and discourages the inevitable, troublesome attachments cultivated by some clients.

Demand peaks on weekends, when prostitutes may service between ten and twenty men a night, but customers can be found anytime, any day of the week. Clients include unaccompanied men as well as groups of teenagers who pile into cars and cruise the streets. The object of this excursion—referred to locally as a *tour de pull*—is to gawk and engage in sexual banter, though observers conceded that it may conclude with the purchase of sex.[27] The women, especially new arrivals, adopt an arduous schedule out of desperation to avoid the madam's wrath.[28] The location of sex work varies. Some women use their own apartments located in the rundown city center while others bring customers to seedy hotels where the madam has made an arrangement. But typically the women station themselves on certain streets and parks, servicing customers in their cars. The Favorita Park on the road to the seaside resort of Mondello, is a principal location, with shifts in the morning, evening, and night. Other busy sites in Palermo include areas along the port and Foro Italico, a harborside promenade, and the streets and piazzas of the old city. Police surveillance and raids can temporarily redirect business to other areas or even other cities. A Sicilian whose volunteer work brings her into contact with immigrants in run-down areas of the old city recounted a telling scene from the late 1990s. One day she met a group of Nigerian women carrying mattresses and bedding material. Her interest piqued by this odd sight, she inquired after their purpose. The women responded matter-of-factly that, owing to a police raid in the eastern Sicilian city of Catania, their compatriots had come to stay with them in Palermo for a while.

Danger and degradation characterize the trafficked woman's life. Given the premium paid for unprotected sex and the pressure to purchase their freedom, prostitutes always run the risk of STDs, and daily sexual relations with up to a dozen men can cause pain and discomfort. Some clients verbally abuse the women, some assault them while attempting to steal their services or earnings. In Favorita Park, youths are known to drive by, pelting the women with refuse. The women defend themselves forcefully; in cooler months, they do not hesitate to go after their assailants with burning branches pulled from the ever-present fire. With little or no previous experience in sex work, the women may be slow to develop the professional stance crucial to managing clients and minimizing risks. Like street prostitutes everywhere, Nigerians in Palermo frequently seek solace or escape in alcohol, drugs, and money.[29] Observers describe prostitutes' lives as degraded. Weeks are passed in an alcoholic haze. Apartments are overstuffed with mattresses, littered with empty bottles, and strewn with discarded clothes.

At the same time, poor and ambitious young women enjoy the novel pleasure of having real money pass through their hands. This can take singular expressions. A Palermitan and long-time observer of immigrant life recalled attending a prostitutes' birthday party together with some Ivorian friends in the mid-1990s.

> It was an unforgettable evening! There were a hundred Nigerian women and maybe ten men. Two of these guys were smitten Italian clients, the others Nigerian muscle. The women drank a lot and danced. They wore fancy designer clothes from elegant shops I would be made to feel unwelcome even entering. The clothes were the best, costing hundreds of dollars and still with the price tags attached! The cake was completely forgotten, the women were totally stoned. Then the party ended abruptly at 10:30—they had to go to work!

What happened the next morning also speaks to the prostitute's mind-set. One of the Ivorians, a photographer, came round to sell the photographs he had taken the night before. But the women, realizing that he could not identify them without their clothes and make-up, reacted in a cagey fashion. "Oh, she's not in," they would say, "but I'll just take that one and give it to her when she comes back. Don't worry, she'll pay you as soon as she returns." The photographer lost a bundle on the event. Commented the Sicilian observer: "They realized that their identities were malleable, that they could take advantage of his ignorance."

The attentions of clients can also offer satisfaction to the women. As elsewhere, the client in Palermo is everyman.[30] He might be the married man or the bachelor, the university student or the baker. A Nigerian prostitute quipped to a female Sicilian social worker that "we get them all, even your boyfriend. If you Italian women had any sense you'd join us on the street and make some money for your troubles!" Like clients everywhere, men in Palermo are drawn to prostitutes by the ease and anonymity of the transaction as well as by the promise of sexual gratification without the complications of mutuality or responsibility. Some grow attached to individual women. These smitten clients might return five minutes after the act, bearing a cup of coffee or some other token of their appreciation. Some men, typically older and for whom the sex act itself appears to be of secondary importance, thrill to the pleasure of basking in the presence of their object of desire. On holidays they bestow jewelry and other gifts of a romantic nature, and some have been known to pay off a sex worker's debts. For prostitutes, such attentions bespeak their desirability and constitute valuable assets. These relations also grant a woman, so often abused as a mere African whore, the opportunity to dominate an Italian man. While some women do eventually leave the street to join an Italian, most manipulate the man and speak of him with contempt in private. Prostitutes occasionally have much younger Italian boyfriends. In these relationships the woman freely goes out with the man, provided that he is a big spender and is not jealous of her clients. As one Nigerian told a social worker, the minute "he interferes with my work, he's gone." Needless to say, the gifts and attentions of clients and boyfriends provoke admiration and jealousy among the women.

WORKING WITH PROSTITUTES

Given the realities of the women's lives, anti-trafficking efforts in Palermo face serious challenges. In recent years a number of projects have taken up the cause in one way or another. Some are ongoing, others defunct or moribund. Some deal exclusively with prostitution and trafficking while others incorporate these issues into a larger agenda. For some, women need to be liberated from the sinful bondage of prostitution while others object to trafficking but uphold a woman's right to sell sex in accordance with Italian law. Some participate in street teams, others run residential homes, and still others attempt to generate interest in the subject among the authorities and the public. The recent commitment to anti-trafficking measures on the part of the European Union and the Italian government has underwritten a flurry of recent (2002–2004) activity. As of 2003, the region of Sicily has a hotline and two associations perform virtually the same work under the provisions of Section 18.[31]

A description of one ongoing project affords a window onto some of the activities and dilemmas faced by anti-trafficking efforts in Palermo. The Project, established in 2001 and authorized under Section 18, is one of the city's better funded and most comprehensive initiatives. The Project offers daily assistance to prostitutes as well as a program for women who wish to leave the street and their exploiters. The effort is run under the auspices of a nation-wide association concerned with marginalized populations like drug addicts, battered women, and AIDS patients. While Project personnel recognize the existence of different forms of sex work among foreigners and Italians and offer assistance to all who request it, their focus is squarely upon Nigerian prostitutes. The Project supports two street teams, each composed of a psychologist, a social worker, and a cultural mediator. The mediators, a man and a woman, are both West Africans and long-time residents of the Sicilian capital. In conception and execution the project has benefited from programs developed by NGOs elsewhere.[32]

Project personnel—who may work on the street or in the office or both—arrange for medical attention and accompany women on routine and emergency visits to the hospital and doctors' offices. They hand out free condoms and air horns, and urge the women to adopt safe practices such as avoiding drunken clients, working in groups, insisting on condom use, and the like. In these ways the teams establish the context for another goal, that of "pulling" the women from the streets. Team members describe the rehabilitation program authorized under Section 18 and tell the women about a special office set up for the purpose.

The realities of trafficking and the volatile behavior of the prostitutes make these tasks extremely difficult. Mediators describe the women as very aggressive, at least initially. They shout, taunt, and even strike at their would-be helpers. When it suits them, they speak insistently in Pidgin English, pretending they cannot understand a word the team utters in Italian, English, and French. Nor do they hide their suspicions. More than once they have rifled through the project vehicle, searching for surveillance equipment (there was none). On one occasion they begged a team to call the police, saying that they had just been robbed. Project personnel, who normally would not call the police because that usually spells trouble for the women, acceded to their request. The police caught the perpetrators and the team handled the paperwork. A member recalled that the women had peeked out from the trees (much of the work occurs in the Favorita Park) to verify that their request had been carried out.

As this story suggests, the prostitutes often put the teams to tests even as they come to depend on them. A female mediator described women who touch and rub up against her, saying they have AIDS. One evening, she arrived and made ready to greet the women gathered in a corner of the park. A prostitute, her face and chest dripping with semen, grabbed her in a tight embrace. The mediator suppressed a strong urge to recoil but instead hugged the woman back. Later the prostitute bragged about how she had emptied the contents of used condoms in order to create a test for the mediator. Commenting on the event, the mediator explained that the sex workers are disgusted with themselves. Because they fear seeing the same disgust in the eyes of others, they attempt to drive them away, in this case by daring them to react with horror. While she would like to wear gloves, the mediator realizes that the women would interpret such a precaution as an indication of their own dirtiness and refuse her assistance.

Under these conditions, cultivating trust requires patience and tact. Little by little the women come to appreciate the teams as reliable and nonjudgmental sources of help and company. A team member recalled how a woman who once tried to strike her later came to her in tears, begging for help after a condom broke. The most outrageous lies cease and a conversation, tentative to be sure, begins. At the hospital, team members learn women's real, as opposed to the professional, names, but preserve the fiction of the pseudonym by pretending not to notice.

In its first three years of operation, the Project managed to convince only a few prostitutes to flee their traffickers.[33] The effort's success instead appears to rest in the daily concrete assistance it offers and in the behavioral change it effects in women. Team members claim that condom use is very common if not the rule on the street now, and they report an extremely low rate of HIV/AIDS. A mediator described the women's new preoccupation with health: "They get sick as soon as they see me. 'Take me for a test,' they say, and we do it." In these ways, by learning how to identify perils and avoid or minimize them, sex workers gain a measure of control over their situation and secure benefits to their physical and mental well-being.[34] Such lessons can have important long-term effects because experienced workers may in turn instruct new recruits and because after repayment many women remain in Italy, supplementing their income with independent sex work.

FORMS OF CONTROL: DEBT PEONAGE AND VIOLENCE

The same profile of limited success is experienced by anti-trafficking initiatives elsewhere in Palermo and indeed across Italy.[35] Discussions in Palermo and the literature suggest that the Nigerian system, specifically the powerful forms of control employed by traffickers, account for these patterns. Highlighted here are debt peonage and threat of violence, family obligations, and supernatural sanctions.

To reiterate, a woman's debt obligation commences when she (or her family) enters into an agreement with a trafficker in Nigeria (called the "sponsor"), pledging to pay for safe passage to Europe from the future earnings of the job she will receive there. The enormous initial debt is augmented by occasional penalties for insubordination or late payment and by inflated deductions for room and board and other expenses. The madam berates unruly women, reminding them of the pact they have entered, and may beat them herself or call in Nigerian male "hitters." For her family back in Nigeria, a woman's failure to uphold the agreement in Italy can result in threats, beatings, and destruction of property. Owing to endemic corruption in Nigeria, families have little chance of resisting the well-funded and well-connected criminal interests involved in trafficking.

The threat of violence is thus an important form of control and may even be the preferred method of some madams.[36] Until she fled an arrest warrant in 2001, Regina was one of Palermo's most feared and successful madams. A somewhat older woman and a former prostitute, Regina fit the profile of the madam. In possession of legal status and enjoying access to capital and to connections in both Nigeria and Italy, she was able to move fellow Nigerians into Palermo. An ambitious operator, she ran women in two locations and sought to gain control over valuable territories. As sponsor, trolley, and madam, she combined roles that often remain separate. Regina's taking on multiple roles, like her penchant for violence, may reflect her ambition and personality, the contours of the street trade in Sicily at that time, or both. Her case also serves as a reminder of the variation and flexibility characteristic of Nigerian trafficking.

In 1997 Regina personally recruited Joy and accompanied her from Benin City. Once in Sicily, Regina took Joy's false passport and put her to work on the streets of Cefalù, a fashionable coastal resort area to the east of Palermo. Regina demanded that Joy produce each month 1,000,000 Lire for the joint and 3,000,000 Lire towards a total debt of 50,000,000 Lire (about US$25,000 at the time). A sadistic manager, Regina tortured Joy, pulling out fingernails and forcing her to stand nude all night on a balcony. She conducted rites, threatening Joy with supernatural reprisals. After she paid her debt in 1999, Joy left to work on her own on the streets on Milan. When she returned to Cefalù in 2001, Regina sought her out and demanded joint money. When Joy refused, Regina threatened her life. In Cefalù and in Palermo, Regina and her female associates accosted Joy, beating her up and stealing from her on several occasions.

At the same time Regina was fighting for supremacy of one of Palermo's most popular venues for open-air commercial sex. But her continued use of force bespoke an inability to impose her will, even within her own house. Rachael, whom she had sponsored the year before, refused to yield earnings and joint money. Neither rites nor threats moved the girl. Exasperated, Regina ordered in two male "hitters." They broke into Rachael's apartment, beat her, and stole a videocassette showing the parents of both women (Rachael and Regina) making vows before a traditional priest.

The plight of Rachael and Joy reminds us of the systematic use of intimidation and violence on the part of madams and their far-flung associates. In her efforts to exploit Rachael and to extract the joint costs from Joy (and from other now-independent prostitutes), Regina engaged in displays of force, often made in public places. That she could ultimately accomplish neither goal suggests the limitations of violence as a management strategy. Of course, Nigerian madams do physically punish recalcitrant women and call for the hitters. But they prefer to send difficult women to colleagues in other cities. And, in line with their strategy of maintaining a low profile, they prefer to avoid unnecessary violence. Excessive use of force poses grave dangers to their business interests, because it attracts the attention of the police and convinces victims that the authorities offer them the best chance of survival and possibly revenge.

In general, trafficked women gain more autonomy over time. While the new recruit is kept under close surveillance, the woman who has regularly paid down the debt for a time is granted more freedom. She may send (more) money to her parents and mail letters home with photographs showing her in beautiful clothes posing next to symbols of European wealth. She may communicate more freely with Italian clients, friends, and social workers. The introduction of the cellular telephone, which enables madams to keep track of women from afar, also has granted the prostitutes unprecedented liberty of movement and communication. Madams in recent years have physically distanced themselves from the women they exploit. In the past, they typically resided with or near the women, demanded frequent installments of the debt, and generally exercised direct control. Police raids and a series of arrests, starting in the late 1990s, however, have made such hands-on management very risky. Madams now reside far from their stable of women, delegating daily affairs to senior prostitutes, or "sisters," while money is transferred electronically or picked up by male couriers. Despite these changes in daily operations, the woman who runs away risks violence to herself and her loved ones in Nigeria. Considering that enrollment in a Section 18 program offers merely the promise of a short-term permit (in all likelihood opening up only the possibility for documented low-wage employment), it is understandable that very few trafficked women flee their traffickers and that those who do enroll in Section 18 programs decline to cooperate with the police. As one prostitute bluntly said to a Project social worker, "I'll leave the street as soon as you offer me as much as I'm making right now."

FORMS OF CONTROL: FAMILY AND NETWORK

Family and network cement the trafficking relationship in several ways. Prostitution abroad offers poor and ambitious young women the possibility to provide for themselves and their families in a way they could never do if they remained at home. As a prostitute expressed it to a member of the Project, "I'm doing this so my daughter won't have to." Friends and family members often act as recruiters, touting the benefits of work in Europe and even arranging for potential recruits to meet with traffickers ("sponsors"). Former prostitutes who become madams have been known to recruit their own sisters, cousins, and family friends to join them in Italy. Consider the case of Augusta. In 1998, at the height of the boom in outdoor prostitution in Palermo, she controlled the services of over a dozen women. Hiding behind a paper mask of pseudonyms and a bogus cultural association, she drew on connections in her native Benin City to recruit and transport women. Like many small firms, Augusta's was a family affair. She sponsored and put to work cousins and siblings. Relying on the bonds of kinship as well as spiritual and physical coercion, she extracted up to 70,000,000 Lire (about US$35,000) per woman. Thus, apart from concerns over physical safety, obligations to family and ambitions to accumulate significant resources guarantee that most Nigerians will remain on the street long enough to repay the debt (reportedly one and one-half to three years), if not longer.

The role of family and network cannot be understood outside the context of gender discrimination and economic problems in Nigeria. In response to a crisis in the early 1980s brought on by the end of the country's oil boom (and exacerbated by endemic corruption), Nigeria agreed to a Structural Adjustment Program (SAP) in 1986. In accepting the loan package, Nigeria adopted a series of neo-liberal measures proposed by the International Monetary Fund and the World Bank, including cutting governmental expenditures, privatization, devaluation of the Nigerian currency (the Naira), freezing wages, and lifting price controls. In the eight or so years in which these measures were in effect, unemployment rose, social services withered, living standards fell, and the numbers of the very poor surged. According to the report[37] commissioned by United Nations Interregional Crime and Justice Research Institute (UNICRI), from the late 1980s emigration, crime, and trafficking for the purposes of sexual exploitation have flourished in Benin City and surrounding Edo State, the area from which most trafficked women come. Young women in particular have faced tremendous obstacles in this environment. While their brothers remain in school, girls' educations come second to caretaking roles within large, often polygynous households. On the labor market, women's employment and earning potential are constrained by gender discrimination and limited educational credentials. Because women bear primary responsibility for children, they have suffered more than men by the decline in social services and economic opportunity; this is especially the case for the poorer women who are most likely to bear children at a young age. Finally, animism and polytheism glorify male ancestors, bolstering the patriarchal system.

Lack of education and the common view that daughters are servants of family interests have worked to channel girls, especially poorer ones, into prostitution, both at home and abroad, from the late 1980s.[38] The possibility of sex work abroad is common knowledge in Benin City. In a survey of almost 1,500 young women, one-third reported being approached with offers of a sojourn outside the country, almost half knew someone who had gone abroad for prostitution, and about the same figure agreed that there were positive benefits to be gained by women engaged in trafficking.[39] Parents, who would have repudiated prostitute daughters in the recent past, have come to tolerate them as a welcome source of income in uncertain times. As a former prostitute in Palermo put it when asked about the attitude of Nigerians to the participation of so many young women in prostitution abroad, "No one asks questions when you are doing well." Given the reality that the surest way for a poor Nigerian to get to Europe and the riches it represents is by resorting to traffickers, the sponsor is viewed as a potential benefactor rather than as a criminal.[40] The figure of the sponsor, like that of the "coyote" who for a fee leads aspiring immigrants across the desert into the United States, may be viewed more as hero than as villain by the aspiring immigrant. In Benin City as in rural Mexico the illegality of the proposed journey amounts to yet another obstacle in the quest to achieve a decent living and ensure a brighter future for one's family.

Like all migrations, the movement of sex workers is facilitated by networks. Women from Edo State predominated among the first generation of prostitutes in Italy; over time, these women have become madams, in turn recruiting and controlling other women. Because most belong to the Bini (or Edo) ethnic group, this population is most closely associated with the trade. (Women from other areas in Nigeria and other local ethnic groups have also entered the trade, but their presence is hard to ascertain because of the prevalence of false identities.) According to Christiana Okojie, "Trafficking is now so ingrained in Edo State, especially in Benin City and its immediate environs, that it is estimated that virtually every Bini family has one member or the other involved in trafficking either as 'victim,' sponsor, madam or trafficker."[41]

In itself, material deprivation does not suffice to account for trafficking; after all, most areas in Nigeria are poor but trafficking is centered in Benin City. The explanation lies instead in the powerful conjunction of need, aspiration for the visible material benefits of the trade, criminal expertise, and the networks whose cumulative effect makes sex work in Europe a very real option for young women.

FORMS OF CONTROL: SUPERNATURAL THREATS

In addition to debt bondage and family obligations, religion acts to keep trafficked women on the streets of Palermo. The contract signed, the sponsor in Nigeria arranges for the woman to swear a sacred oath before a traditional shrine or celebrant in which she pledges, on pain of supernatural retribution, to honor her debt and to keep secret the identities and methods of her traffickers. The ritual involves retaining a woman's bodily substances—pubic hair, nail clippings, even blood—to ensure compliance. In Italy, madams routinely threaten recalcitrant women (and their families) with a spiritual reprisal. They may remind them of the oath taken at home, and some madams tend shrines in their apartments and conduct rites themselves.

Various terms are used to refer to animistic religious practices common to West Africa. According to published sources, social workers, scholars, and police investigators refer to "voodoo," a term also employed by some women. The women themselves tend to speak of the "sacred oath," as do some observers. With regard to the location and execution of the rites, there appears to be some variation, with rites being administered both in Italy and Nigeria by madams and by traditional priests (or individuals claiming such status). According to Francesco Prina, rites were administered in Italy through the early 1990s but are now conducted first in Nigeria then repeated in Italy. Observers agree that the rites reinforce the subjugation of the women to traffickers. While some Western observers maintain that the women are spellbound by African magic, investigators and scholars have come to appreciate the complexity of the phenomenon. Prina notes that women feel as bound by taking an oath before family and community as they do by any supernatural obligation, and we think of the case of Rachael, whose filial and sacred duties were cleverly fused in the videotaped rite involving her, her parents, and the parents of her madam.[42]

Another perspective comes from Rijk Van Dijk, a cultural anthropologist who worked with the "voodoo team" established by Dutch police to combat Nigerian trafficking in the Netherlands.[43] It is important to note that he spoke with women who had turned themselves in to the Dutch authorities rather than remain on the street. The women very rarely described their religious experiences in Nigeria as "voodoo." Rites at traditional shrines sealed the bond between them and their recruiters, they averred.[44] The men promised to procure necessary documents and tickets and settle them in Europe while the women vowed to repay the resulting debt. The women experienced the rites as empowering, safeguarding their journey and enabling them to partake of the magic of European-style mobility and wealth. Once in the Netherlands, however, the women experienced a coercive mix of violence and "occult intimidation" at the hands of their madams and male enforcers, especially when they failed to perform as expected. It was this form of threat they came to call "voodoo." Comments Van Dijk:

> The implication is that "voodoo" denotes a kind of "inauthentic" ritual, not performed on the girls' behalf, not with their own but solely with the operators' commercial interests in mind, and not performed by ritual specialists who would want to safeguard their public status and prestige. "Voodoo" became synonymous with spiritual entrapment and with being policed through occult means by their madams and pimps in every move they made.[45]

Police and social workers in Palermo agree that madams routinely make reference to or reenact oaths, and that this supernatural threat is an important part of the subjugation of trafficked women. Difference of opinion does exist regarding the nature and efficacy of the rites. Sicilians explain it in terms of custom and culture, citing the prevalence of animism in West Africa. As one put it, "voodoo is as natural to them as Catholicism is to us." Africans are divided over the nature of ritual but agree that the trafficked women believe in it. One immigrant mediator described how the oath binds "like steel" until the debt is paid. Formerly enrolled in a nursing program and a firm believer in the reality of magic, she recalled seeing prostitutes slow in paying off the debt coming down with mysterious complaints and conditions. She asserted that Italian doctors, ignorant of the power of magic, remain bewildered by women's symptoms as medical tests reveal nothing.

The other Project mediator offered a different interpretation. According to him, all West Africans, from peasant to professor, believe in the power of voodoo, fetishes, and other forms of animism. Like Van Dijk, he distinguished true from false animism, the former being beneficial the latter a perversion inspired by evil intent. According to him, immediately before their departure for Europe prospective prostitutes are subject to a "fake" ritual in which they pledge to repay their debts on pain of terrible retribution. Their handlers do not take them to a real priest or temple, because legitimate religious figures would not permit such a sacrilege. In Palermo, madams present themselves as voodoo priestesses, making daily ceremonies at the shrines they maintain at home. But as false religion, the traffickers' voodoo is without true efficacy. In support of the interpretation, the mediator noted that with a single exception (in all probability brought on by extreme stress), he has never seen mysterious behavior or illness among any of the women (including those he has helped leave the street). Yet, the prostitutes actually believe they will go crazy if they break their oath. When he tries to calm their fears, they object, "But you're African, you have to believe us!" He attributes this response to ignorance, but it is also conceivable that such utterances are intended to cultivate the image of an all-powerful of control from which they are unable to escape. (We return to the notion of strategic claims of total victimhood later.) Another indication that religion is more complex than imagined by most observers comes from a former prostitute. According to her, women commonly possess amulets and other items thought to confer benefit or protection, suggesting again an ambiguous relation of the women to religious practice.

Whatever their interpretation of the role of religion, few who work with prostitutes would disagree with the statement of a West African observer:

> But it's just too easy. You could put poison in somebody's drink and then claim it's because of voodoo, but you can't really harm somebody at a distance. If there really were this power around, man we'd be rich! Instead we're poor and we see our women on the streets here. That really hurts.

In sum, Nigerian prostitutes struggle with the combined pressures of repaying an enormous debt to violent criminals with powerful transnational connections, family obligations, and fear of religious sanction—all in a foreign country whose language and ways they little understand. These conditions account for the low incidence of women leaving their madams and their reluctance to aid police investigations (even after their debts are discharged). The alternating aggressive and needy behavior with which they confront street teams likewise stems from these terrible pressures. Under these conditions, Project personnel, while not quite abandoning the hope of assisting women in fleeing their traffickers, realize that the surest benefit they can bring involves the daily contact and medical and other assistance. In 2004, an immigrant cultural mediator described his changing understanding of the Project's role. In the first years, he thought his efforts might well incur the wrath of madams and their associates, but it was a risk he was willing to accept in light of the human tragedy unfolding before him. Now he realizes that the women will not flee their exploiters until the Project can offer substantial resources; in the meantime, traffickers tolerate the Project as its services ensure the health (and therefore profitability) of their victims. As another Project worker put it, "our task is to reduce the damage [associated with a phenomenon we cannot control]."

AFTER THE DEBT

A few women, finding unbearable their humiliation on the street and their subjugation to the madam, run away. Responding to our queries regarding the formidable control of the madam and her associates, a former prostitute rebutted, "What do you think, that you're controlled all the time? One day you can go in the front door of the tobacconist's shop, leave by the back door, and you're gone." But women who flee on their own always run the risk of being caught, punished, and put to work again. Some women find refuge with the police or an association, and a few seek to be repatriated. In other cases a boyfriend-admirer-client or social workers engineer an escape.

Given the strong web of threats and obligations binding them to traffickers, the majority remain on the street until their debt is paid—a period of one and a half to three years by all accounts. At this point some return to Nigeria and others remain in Italy.[46] Once free of systematic exploitation, the Nigerian woman confronts the challenges of getting by with limited competence in Italian, few marketable skills, and a checkered past. For most, this means low pay and long hours as undocumented house cleaners and caregivers to the infirm and elderly. Convinced of the moral imperative and health benefits of a new life, a woman may persevere, holding down several jobs. A religious awakening may also firm her resolve. The church, usually a Protestant denomination, offers an explanation for past errors, a design for a better future, and possibly a supportive community—an important resource for someone who may have lost her place in a family by virtue of retiring from a lucrative business. The woman quoted above, active in an association and intent on pursuing higher education in Italy, described her involvement with a series of religious institutions. "I feel that I need more spirituality in my life," she summarized. Another woman, who spent two years on the street paying a debt before entering a church-sponsored rehabilitation program, also referred to the power of faith, and observed that a reason that active prostitutes are so different from others is their loss of a moral compass:

> They just don't think. No one acts like this in ordinary life. . . . They may be suffering inside, but they don't know how to express themselves. They don't trust anybody, they're closed inside. They've lost their faith and any hope in themselves.

Not all find sustenance in religion and individual liberty. Others, unaccustomed to the long hours of domestic work and frustrated by low pay, return to the street. Through occasional sex work she can meet expenses, purchase the goods to which she has become accustomed, and perhaps send money home to Nigeria. A veteran of the streets, she insists on condom use and monitors her health. Her own master, she follows her own schedule, declines obnoxious clients, and retains her own earnings, although she like Joy may have to render a fee for her place on the sidewalk.

Still other women may seize the opportunity to amass their fortune. They may become full-time independent prostitutes like Joy or they may receive a stake in their madam's affairs by serving as a daily manager, perhaps continuing sex work at the same time. And, reinvesting the money so earned in new recruits, they become madams in their own right. As the case of Augusta demonstrates, the aspiring madam may prefer to recruit her own family members, a practice that ensures tractable workers and keeps wealth within the family.

Because most Nigerians hold expired or forged papers, the quest for legal status looms regardless of the path chosen. Faking domestic employment and taking advantage of the occasional amnesty offered by the Italian government is one option. Rehabilitation programs authorized under Section 18 offer another. As noted previously, programs grant trafficking victims a series of protections and possibilities for a future outside of sex work. Of the two ways of entering the program—denouncing the exploiters and aiding a police inquiry or simply reporting the fact of being trafficked and enrolling with an association—most choose the second option, to the consternation of the police.[47] Nigerian women, fearing reprisals, favor the social path to the permit and usually enter programs upon or near completion of their debt. For them, Section 18 has become another means to legal status. Once a woman has entered such a program, she is expected to renounce prostitution, complete a rehabilitation program (often including a stay at a residential center), and undertake job training. Once she has fulfilled these obligations and held a job for a period, her temporary permit may be replaced with a regular one. These steps bring Project personnel into frequent, often demanding contact with Nigerians.

ANTI-TRAFFICKING DILEMMAS

There exists some variation among Project personnel with regard to the nature of trafficking and the legitimacy of prostitution, of course, but experience on the street and repeated encounters in the office with Nigerians engender recognition of the complexities of the situation. A female Italian social worker, for example, described how she viewed the women as total victims of sexual slavery when she began at the Project. Now she understands that most were not duped into prostitution (though they were surely surprised by the brutality of their exploitation in Italy) and that they regard the Section 18 program as a convenient means to legal status. Like workers at other anti-trafficking efforts in the city, she complains that the women routinely alter the details of their stories, miss appointments, refuse to answer questions about their trafficking experiences, and do not disguise their view of Project personnel as irritating, bureaucratic obstacles standing in the way of a permit. Furthermore, some women continue to engage in sex work, despite having pledged to stop (a requirement for enrollment), occasioning angry calls to the Project from the police.

The relationship between Project personnel and the women is characterized by tension and accommodation, two instances of which are noted here. Nigerian women all offer the same story: That they are misled by offers of a good job in Europe and subsequently coerced into prostitution. With time Project workers come to realize (as research in Nigeria also has shown) that most women choose to enter pacts with traffickers, albeit in the context of widespread gender and class inequalities. The women's nearly identical stories should therefore be viewed more as ritual assertions of innocence than as statements of fact. In other words, the women seek to enhance their eligibility for Section 18 programs by engaging in what Frank Boven, Dina Siegel, and Damián Zaitich call "ethnic reputation manipulation," by implying or claiming to be completely victimized by traffickers wielding awesome powers, including supernatural ones.[48]

Second, as noted earlier it is not uncommon for women enrolled in the program to return to the street. Project workers are frustrated by this pattern; by selling sex on the street, the women are breaking their word, exposing themselves to disease, and risking deportation should the police catch them. At the same time, they acknowledge that Section 18 programs provide so little in the way of job security and income that such an outcome is all but inevitable. Project personnel do appreciate the difficulties the women experience as they attempt to make a living in the low-paying and dead-end jobs that are offered in the program and that await the women in the future. Viewing the women as scared, in desperate need, and manipulative by turns, they continue to offer advice and assistance, hoping to reduce the damage once more.

Section 18 certainly represents an important advance over the former practice of deporting foreign prostitutes lacking legal status. As the Palermo case shows, the program treats the women as victims of trafficking rather than as illegal aliens, and offers a range of supports as well as the possibility of legal status. As an anti-trafficking measure, however, Section 18 has yielded modest gains in the judicial arena owing to the preference of Nigerians for the social protection route and their reluctance to testify against their exploiters. Job training and subsidies are crucial to attract participants and to help those enrolled make the difficult adjustments of the first two years, but social workers and legal consultants complain that lack of funding hampers the effectiveness of the program.

For former prostitutes, the future does not appear bright. In chapter 3 we saw how limited job opportunities, employer preferences, and legal status channeled many immigrants into domestic work. Over time, Filipinos and other predominantly female domestic worker populations have secured better pay and work conditions, in Palermo or in the north, through job performance and networks composed of co-ethnics and affluent employers. Although they have confronted obstacles with regard to family formation and complain of being limited to domestic work, they have achieved a position of high status within the sector's hierarchy. Former prostitutes, lacking skills and relevant work experience, find themselves at the bottom of the hierarchy of domestics. They face the difficult task of remaking their lives while supporting themselves (and possibly continuing to contribute to family at home) through a series of poorly paid, part-time jobs. Nor are their previous associations, for the most part made up of co-nationals involved in criminality, of assistance in this quest. Without the networks of family, friends, and employers enjoyed by other immigrants, Nigerian ex-prostitutes have a harder time moving up within the domestic sector (like the career domestic populations) or attempting occupational and geographical movement (like the men who sought refuge in the sector only to move on once they received legal status). Although these deficits may be partly counterbalanced by the resources of Section 18, offering limited job opportunities and a small Nigerian population apparently focused on criminal pursuits, Palermo would appear an unfavorable location for the integration of program participants. These challenges are certainly not confined to the Sicilian capital, however. As studies[49] elsewhere in Italy suggest, securing steady legal employment remains the biggest problem for Section 18 participants.

THE MORE THINGS CHANGE

In Palermo and indeed across Italy, street prostitution and trafficking have come under increased scrutiny by police, media, and NGOs and other organizations. As a consequence of these efforts, the number of women involved appears to have declined in recent years, and they no longer offer sex quite as openly as in the 1990s. However, the Palermo case suggests that trafficking is far from being eliminated. The appetite for paid sex among Italian men shows no sign of slackening. In a context of thorough-going gender discrimination, the disintegration of civil society, economic uncertainty, and well-trodden pathways to Europe, numbers of young women and their families continue to convince themselves that the imagined benefits of a European sojourn outweigh the rumored risks of entering into a pact with powerful sponsors. Barring a significant economic upsurge in Nigeria together with corresponding opportunities for women, many poor young women will continue to offer themselves up to traffickers.

In addition to efficient mechanisms for indebting and controlling vulnerable women, the success of traffickers rests on the ability to operate with seeming impunity in Nigeria. Despite a 2000 agreement between Italy and Nigeria and despite the recent introduction of anti-trafficking (and anti-prostitution) laws in Edo State, very little headway has been made against trafficking. As the UNICRI report observes, not a single individual has been convicted of trafficking in Nigeria (as of 2003). True, parents have taken traffickers to court, but not to levy charges of sexual exploitation. Because parents sometimes pay for part of the passage up front, when a daughter fails to gain entry to Europe some angry parents actually sue the traffickers for failure to uphold contractual obligations. Others take the matter up in traditional courts. Nigerian women repatriated by Italian authorities routinely disappear within hours of arrival from the reception center in Lagos, only to seek out their traffickers in an attempt to return to Italy. Barring a sea change in Nigerian law enforcement and economic conditions, the Italian police will be limited to making business more difficult for traffickers.

As police are only too aware, traffickers have a keen understanding of the Italian (and European Union) system and the flexibility to adapt to challenges and opportunities. When we returned to Palermo early in the summer of 2004 after an absence of a little more than a year, we learned of several new strategies. One involves exploiting the right to file for political asylum granted to foreigners by the Italian government. A small but increasing number of Nigerian women now claim to have escaped from Liberia, the Ivory Coast, even Nigeria itself—they select a plausible refugee identity depending on current media reports of political turmoil and violence in West Africa. Supposedly having fled for their lives, the women assert they destroyed all proof of identity in an effort at self-preservation. Applicants to asylum status gain the right to reside in Italy until their case is decided in Rome. Given the enormous caseload in Palermo alone—almost 1,000 cases were pending in 2004—applicants are assured of legal status for at least one year. This legal ruse enables the women to sell sex with impunity because prostitution itself is not a crime.[50]

Other changes concern daily operations. As noted earlier, for fear of arrest madams have all but disappeared from circulation. Whereas previously they lived either with or in close proximity to their women, monitored them, and personally demanded payment, today madams keep their distance. They move frequently, residing elsewhere in Italy, in Nigeria, or in Spain (an important transit point for traffickers). In their absence, Nigerian male "uncles" and "papas" periodically collect cash, while prostitutes also send money to madams or intermediaries through money transfer services such as Western Union. A senior woman, preferably a relative of the madam, oversees living and working arrangements. On the street, hired male Sicilian helpers chauffeur the women from place to place, bring food and drink, and alert the women to the presence of police patrols. To reduce the effectiveness of police searches, the women no longer reside in large groups but instead stay in dispersed apartments. Overall, the madam and her accomplices have understood that overbearing control and excessive use of force, at least in Italy, can drive women into the hands of police and associations.

Traffickers have also granted women more liberty while cultivating a sense of obligation bolstered by fear. According to one social worker, particularly important in this regard is the period from arrival and the filing of an asylum claim to the beginning of work on the street. The woman comes to accept her situation as she sees the money flow all around her. So while she may appear to be freer than before, the Nigerian prostitute will just as surely repay her debt on the streets, and if she is clever and ambitious, in time she may well become a madam. Such tactics, lamented the social worker, have made it all but impossible for his team to pose a serious threat to the Nigerian system in Palermo. While he used to worry about his safety he now realizes that the traffickers regard him as providing free health and other services to their women rather than posing a threat to the business of trafficking.

In Palermo, as elsewhere, the basic components of the system have remained intact. The flexibility of the network structure has permitted traffickers to profit from street prostitution year after year. Increasing police surveillance has raised the costs of doing business—a cost passed on to the women in the form of escalating debts—and it has forced the traffickers to adopt new tactics but has not halted the trade in women. Given the impunity with which traffickers operate in Nigeria, the many-sided control they exercise over women, and the buoyant market for sex in the West, their continued success seems likely.

A DIFFERENT KIND OF SUBSIDY

Because it involves violence, coercion, and human rights abuses, trafficking is sometimes referred to as a modern form of slavery. Media reports on the subject feature teenage girls, duped into the trade, held captive, and forced into a hell of relentless sex with strangers. From this unambiguous perspective, trafficked women are forced into the sex trade, slaves who must be set free. The involvement of Nigerian criminal gangs and the terrible conditions experienced by the prostitutes described in this chapter are beyond dispute, but regarding the women as passive or total victims masks a complex reality. As Marjan Wijers has remarked on the basis of over a decade of work on behalf of trafficked women in the Netherlands, we must avoid the common view of trafficked women as:

> weak, stupid or passive victims. On the contrary, a great many end up in this position because they do not want to accept the limitations of the situation, because they are enterprising, courageous and willing to take initiatives to improve their living conditions and those of their families. But somewhere in the process they get trapped.[51]

For the Nigerians whose plight is the subject of this account, the trap involves coercion, exploitation, psychological trauma, violence, STDs, and substance abuse. An important factor in their subjugation involves ritualized forms of control, even if the issue has proven more complex than initially thought. Despite being trapped in an exploitative relationship for the duration of the debt, the women struggle to exercise some autonomy, as their at-times contentious dealings with Project personnel show. While anti-trafficking projects lack the resources to convince the women to leave the street, they offer valuable medical assistance and promote strategies for identifying and containing risky situations. Their debt paid, some women move out of sex work, but their prospects for a satisfying integration appear dim, even with the assistance that is now available through Section 18 and other initiatives. Others choose to stay on the street or attempt to profit from others as madams or their assistants. The future possibilities, constraints, and experiences of those remaining in the trade will in large measure be shaped by the evolution of co-national criminal networks, police activity, and the changing contours of the market for commercial sex.

Each night in the Sicilian capital, Benin City and Palermo are joined in so many cold, purchased, and unequal embraces. Nigerian prostitutes and their Sicilian clients are participants in a rapidly expanding, global industry.[52] Over the past two decades, the sex trade has proliferated, incorporating new markets, new technologies, and the increased mobility of products, consumers, and workers. While the industry promises gratification to all tastes, the principal consumers are heterosexual men who prize variety, beauty, and youth in purchased female entertainers and sex partners. If sex sells, nothing sells like commercial sex. In 1996 alone, Americans spent an estimated U.S. $9 billion on telephone sex, lap dancing, massage parlors, pornography, live-sex shows, prostitution, and sundry Internet services.[53] Sex tourists spend billions of dollars annually in Thailand, the Dominican Republic, Sri Lanka, Cuba, and other destinations where poverty, warm weather, and the complicity of local officials permit the unfettered pursuit of male fantasies.[54] At the same time hundreds of thousands of young women cross regional and international borders to serve as dancers, hostesses, and prostitutes from Tokyo to Amsterdam to New York.

These women enter sex work for much the same reasons that others have traveled to accept jobs as caretakers and maids.[55] Confronted with diminishing opportunities at home, they seek passage to countries with notable demand for women's labor, especially in the service sector. Some women arrive independently, others avail themselves of the services of smugglers, and some are trafficked. All bring an amalgam of hope, desperation, ignorance, and calculation to their journeys. Some foreigners may be found in the upper reaches of the sex market, exercising considerable control over their situations and earning hefty fees as exclusive call girls or escorts. But most immigrant prostitutes operate at the lowest levels —on the street, in sex clubs, and in shop windows—where money is scarce and dependency, isolation, and danger gather as constant companions. As Licia Brussa has observed in the case of Western Europe, the poor and even hazardous living and working conditions confronting most foreign sex workers are not so much a result of trafficking, which involves few women; rather, they stem from restrictive immigration policies and characteristics of the sector. Lacking resources and desperate to gain entry or residence in another country, women are especially vulnerable to the depredations of criminals and entrepreneurs who promise permits and high-paying employment.[56]

The recent proliferation of commercial sex, much of it very cheap, would appear to contradict important strides toward gender equality in word and deed in the West and elsewhere. Freed to an unprecedented degree from traditional restraints (and protections) of family, custom, and ideology, women are free as never before to enter the market, where the most disadvantaged have found they can always find a buyer for use of their bodies.

NOTES

1. Other authors have faced similar problems. Okojie (2003: 29), for example, describes how formerly trafficked women repatriated to Nigeria often responded to researchers by demanding money in exchange for information, refusing to provide details of their experiences, and even denying having been involved in trafficking.

2. The IOM (see www.iom.int) publishes a newsletter on trafficking issues, has produced a series of reports, and actively works with the United Nations and others in anti-trafficking efforts. Di Cortemiglia (2003: 7–9) describes the framework in the EU. The Palermo Convention is described at United Nations Office on Drugs and Crime website (www.unodc.org/palermo).

3. For discussions and definitions, see ICMPD 1999; OSCE 1999; and the United Nations Office on Drugs and Crime website.

4. This according to Justice and Home Affairs, European Commission (2001).

5. Competing views on prostitution also have a bearing on views of trafficked women. Many governments, especially those outside of Western Europe from which many prostitutes originate, define prostitution as a crime. Some feminists describe prostitution as a heinous form of patriarchal exploitation. From either perspective, prostitution is condemned and prostitutes need to be saved or reformed. In contrast, others defend the right of individual women (and men) to engage in what they term "sex work." From this perspective, prostitution is understood as a form of labor deserving recognition in the form of rights and respect rather than as a debased identity—as in the common "whore" stereotype. We acknowledge that few women would have chosen prostitution or stripping if other options were available, that most encounter hardship and humiliation, and that few dare identify themselves as sex workers. That said, we have elected to use sex work as a synonym for prostitution because the term underscores the variability of women's (and men's) engagement within the sector, which includes services as diverse as street prostitution, lap dancing, and telephone sex, and which can range from a temporary pursuit to a career, and exist as a part- or full-time occupation (Kempadoo 1998).

6. Sources consulted include: Ambrosini 2002; DIA 2000, 2003a, 2003b; ICMPD 1999; Okojie 2003; OSCE 1999; Prina 2003; and Transcrime 2002.

7. It remains unclear whether, and to what extent, Nigerian traffickers are linked to larger, pre-existing co-national criminal organizations. From humble beginnings as international drug-runners in the early 1980s, Nigerian criminal groups have expanded and diversified their activities. They engage in credit card and other fraud, sale and forgery of documents, the infamous Nigerian "business letters," and money laundering. They also move considerable quantities of heroin and cocaine into Europe (Sands 2002: 7). The money trail suggests that Nigerian groups, like their counterparts across Europe, have been drawn recently to the high profits and low risks of trafficking women (relative to the consequences for trafficking in arms and drugs). According to the Italian police investigations (Prina 2003), madams reinvest some of the earnings into their business, sometimes by means of a rotating savings club. Other funds are openly remitted to Nigeria for such legal use as house construction or businesses. Madams (and associates) also purchase legitimate businesses in Italy. Phone centers and money transfer franchises are favored as they facilitate the movement of money; also purchased are African-style grocery stores and beauty parlors, these last among the first immigrant businesses in Palermo. Finally, cash, picked up by couriers, is used to buy drugs, particularly cocaine for sale on the European and U.S. markets. This business in cocaine would seem to implicate the existing Nigerian crime groups in the prostitution racket. The exact configuration of the trade in prostitutes and drugs is not known; if such ties

do in fact exist, the nature of collaboration no doubt varies given the flexibility and variation inherent in the network organization.

8. The low estimate comes from Carchedi et al. 2000: 112, and high from Covre with Paradiso 2000.

9. These figures come from CENSIS 2000: 4. Another study, this one conducted in the Milan area in 1998, estimates almost two million encounters annually with street prostitutes (Leonini 1999a: 27). Buzzi (1998: 111) found that 12.5 percent of young men polled had visited a prostitute and nearly two-thirds would not rule out a future encounter (cited in Leonini 1999a: 23).

10. The quotation comes from Colombo 1999a: 47.

11. Colombo 1999b: 156.

12. Campani (2000) distinguishes three types of prostitution: street prostitution; prostitution "hidden" or camouflaged by more acceptable occupations such as dancer; and call girls.

13. We have drawn on Gibson 1993, 1999.

14. Observers and prostitutes' organizations, such as the Comitato per i Diritti Civili delle Prostitute (Committee for the Civil Rights of Prostitutes), judge the law an improvement over the former system of state-regulated brothels and mandatory registration. Yet they point out that it marginalizes prostitutes, depriving them of full rights as workers and citizens, and call for a complete decriminalization of the sector.

15. See, for example, the exposé by Lombezzi (1998). According to Giovanna Campani (2001), the mainstream Italian media, though it expresses a range of views, overall promotes a disturbing image of immigration through a focus on poverty, disorder, and crime. Foreigners are commonly portrayed as exotic, destitute, and inclined to criminality, and the image of the black woman as prostitute has gained currency recently. "Over the last few years, the connection between migration and criminality has become increasingly stressed by the media, to the extent that it has become a national obsession" (Campani 2001: 48).

16. See, for example, Ambrosini 2002; Covre with Paradiso 2000; and Campani 2000.

17. The Comitato per i Diritti Civili delle Prostitute is located in Pordenone (see note 14).

18. Examples are given in Carchedi et al. 2000.

19. The efforts are progressive in the sense that they represent a move away from the former pattern of deportation. As the Transcrime (2002) report notes, however, there is no law specifically against trafficking per se and Italian police must draw on a number of parts of the criminal code to prosecute.

20. Albano 2002: 6.

21. The office, created by a decree form the Ministry of the Interior, is officially called the Sezione Criminalità Extracomunitaria e Prostituzione.

22. Estimates for the late 1990s range from the improbably low figure of twenty to thirty offered by a national survey of prostitution (Carchedi et al. 2000: 116) to the more realistic 200 offered by police to 300 to 500 offered by head of the first association to actually involve itself with foreign sex workers. Estimates given by police and associations in 2003 and in 2004 ranged from fifty to one hundred.

23. Daniele Billittieri, personal communication, April 2003.

24. While prostitution in the Sicilian capital takes many forms and exhibits an international character, it certainly cannot match smaller northern cities such Verona or Brescia for volume and variety. In contrast to the meager offerings in Sicily, northern areas boast a variety of nationalities working the street, a lengthy roster of call girls, sex clubs of every sort, and a full range of escort services (Leonini 1999a; Paradiso with Corve 2000; Prina 2003).

25. See note 6.

26. In the early years of the trade, women were flown directly from Lagos to Rome. In the wake of the scandal at the Italian Embassy in Lagos, where officials were caught selling visas, traffickers have adopted ever more circuitous air routes into Europe. They have also developed land routes. This middle passage through Africa carries its own perils, including border checks, violence, and prostitution (Prina 2003).

27. This is similar to the *puttan tour* described for Milan by Colombo (1999a) though the Milanese young appear to be more interested in actually buying sex.

28. When an observer noted with horror having seen prostitutes so young they had yet to develop breasts, we asked if virgins and extremely young girls commanded higher prices (as is usually reported). She responded that initially the girls are so terrified they will accept prices far below those offered by their older co-workers. Other observers say that clients desire young girls in part because they believe they will be less likely to be infected with the HIV virus.

29. Examples can be found in Lever and Dolnick 2000; O'Connell Davidson 1998; and O'Neill and Baberet 2000.

30. Discussions with social workers and former prostitutes in Palermo, email exchanges with observers elsewhere in Italy, and scholarship on clients—see Leonini 1999b; Lever and Dolnick 2000; Monto 2000; and O'Connell Davidson 1998—lead us to believe that clients in Sicily are similar to those across Europe and America in their behavior and motivations.

31. As of 2003–2004, an informal anti-trafficking network, drawing on between five and ten entities of local and international scope, had been formed with the intention of coordinating messages if not activities.

32. The best known of these is TAMPEP (Transnational AIDS/STD Prevention among Migrant Prostitutes in Europe). TAMPEP was founded in 1993 by organizations in the Netherlands, Germany, and Italy (Brussa 1998) to address the challenges presented by foreign sex workers. TAMPEP offices monitor the industry, cultivate ties to local health authorities, provide a range of legal, medical, and practical services, and make available information about STDs written in the workers' own languages. TAMPEP has also developed techniques for reaching the target audience. Cultural mediators, for example, are trained professionals who share the ethnic or national background of the target population. Mediators seek to communicate across linguistic and cultural divides, promoting safe sex practices and regular medical attention. Peer educators are practicing sex workers who serve as group leaders, imparting knowledge and influencing behavior. (For current initiatives, see www.tampep.com.)

33. Team members gave figures ranging from none to a few while the director claimed a higher figure. He failed to mention that his figure included women who

had been transferred as a safety precaution to Palermo from areas in northern Italy.

34. In her study of TAMPEP efforts in Turin in northern Italy, Wallman (2001) analyzes how such programs help prostitutes manage risk.

35. Personnel working at another association in Palermo offering virtually the same services report similar successes and frustrations. For accounts of anti-trafficking initiatives elsewhere in Italy see Abbatecola 2002; Maluccelli 2002; and Prina 2003.

36. Italian women also face dangers when they take up sex work. In conversations in 2003, several observers brought up the recent murder of a Palermo prostitute; they attributed her death either to a client or to trouble caused by her son, a known drug addict. But the need to work unremittingly on the street for exploiters in possession of more strength, money, and connections makes foreign prostitutes particularly vulnerable. As an associational representative noted, an Italian sex worker has identity papers, friends and family members, accounts with the power company and so on, and often is her own master. If she goes missing somebody will notice and ask questions. A trafficked Nigerian, in contrast, holds fake identity papers, has no family or real friends here, and associates daily with violent criminals. She can disappear—he left no doubt that it happens—and no one would know.

37. We have cited this report under the name of the lead researcher, Christiana Okojie (2003).

38. Bamgbose (2002) describes prostitution as a thriving business in Nigerian cities and notes that adolescent females predominate; parents, once horrified at the thought of a daughter prostitute, have come to accept it a means of generating income. In her account of prostitution in Benin City, Francisca Asowa-Omorodion (2000) notes that economic motives compel young women to engage in sex work; a common scenario is for a teenager to become pregnant and turn to prostitution as a means of supporting herself and her child. Outside the realm of prostitution per se, exchanging sex for favors is far from unknown in Benin City. Omorodion (1993) reports that female traders routinely engage in extramarital affairs, at least partly motivated by pursuit of diverse gifts; and Temin et al. (1999) report that teenagers are sexually active and that economic motivations figure prominently in sexual decisions of teenage girls.

39. Okonofua et al. 2004: 1321–22.

40. It is true that some women, particularly in the early 1990s, may have been duped into the trade. But most, especially from the mid-1990s when the reality of much touted "good job" abroad was known, knew they would be selling sex in Europe; what they could not anticipate was the cruelty and violence of the system.

41. Okojie 2003: 43.

42. Prina 2003: 26, 28.

43. In the mid-1990s, Dutch authorities were perplexed to find that young female Nigerians who had filed for asylum were disappearing from care facilities and turning up in squalid illegal brothels operated by co-nationals. Once in police custody or back in their foster homes, the women acted strangely, going into fits and expressing an urgent need to return to their exploiters. Inquiries made it clear that the traffickers had figured out that under the Dutch system, unaccompanied

minors are granted asylum much more readily than adults, and had utilized this feature to bring many very young girls into the Dutch sex market. According to police, the criminals employed black magic to turn their young victims into zombies totally under their control. These revelations led to a public outcry and parliamentary debate over trafficking, and in 1999 a "Voodoo team" was created in the national police force to confront the problem (Van Dijk 2001).

44. In this case the individual men who would also transport and sell the women, another example of the flexibility of the Nigerian system.

45. Van Dijk 2001: 572.

46. It is unclear just where the women end up after they have finished paying the debt. Most observers in Palermo suggest that the women remain in Italy, at least for some time; there is little to draw them back to Nigeria and in Italy they have the opportunity to gain legal status and earn additional money. Other observers, in contrast, say the women return as there is little to hold them in Italy. Because the women typically enter Italy under a false name, there would seem to be little chance of tracking these movements with precision.

47. Police in Palermo describe having Nigerian women on the brink of providing testimony only to watch them decline at the last minute. Yet they have succeeded in indicting several madams and their associates (they are currently fugitives), in part on the basis of testimony given by victims of trafficking. In the case of applications for Section 18 protection through the social path, police use their discretionary power, interviewing all applicants in an attempt to elicit information regarding traffickers.

48. With regard to the case of Nigerian prostitutes in the Netherlands, the authors suggest that by promoting a view of the women as completely controlled by rites—"voodooization"—authorities downplayed the manifest economic and social motivations of the women and inadvertently constructed a compelling narrative that women and their advocates could utilize in asylum requests (Boven, Siegel, and Zaitich 2003: 32–33).

49. Examples include Abbatecola 2002 and Maluccelli 2002.

50. Claims to asylum are made in one of two ways. As the result of a routine police sweep of the street, a woman may land in a detention center (*centro di permanenza temporaneo*), awaiting identification by the Nigerian authorities and probable deportation. High-priced Sicilian lawyers have begun to appear in these out of the way centers, requesting the inalienable right of their female clients to file for asylum. For observers, this practice demonstrates the financial muscle of the traffickers and shows a powerful commitment to their investments in the women. A far less costly method involves a woman appearing alone and seeking assistance from an NGO, association, or private legal consultant. The leader of one association described how Nigerian women, evidently new to the country, have come to her office, insisting on filing for asylum. When she carefully explains the application procedure and warns that false claims are met with deportations, the women wave off such matters and say they only need a year or two with the status of applicant. While all association representatives realize that the system and perhaps they themselves are being used, opinions differ as how to respond. (Much of a May 2004 meeting of the anti-trafficking network hinged on the asylum question and relations with the police.) Some associations have stopped assisting

asylum applicants altogether. Others continue to help, explaining that their duty is to help people and that of the authorities to ascertain the integrity of the applicant's claims. They struggle, in other words, to balance their responsibility toward individuals in need with a broader anti-trafficking mandate. The police, needless to say, take a dim view indeed of any activity that materially aids traffickers.

51. Wijers 1998: 77.

52. Accounts of the contemporary commercial sex industry include: Kempadoo and Doezema 1998; Kempadoo 1999; Vanwesenbeeck 2001; Weitzer 2000a.

53. Weitzer 2000b: 1.

54. For a discussion of female sex tourists, see O'Connell Davidson and Taylor 1998.

55. Maluccelli (2002) and Gülçür and İlkkaracan (2002) provide good analyses of the motivations of women who enter sex work. The many constraints channeling so many women into sex work, as well as the many dangers of the occupation, call into question the common distinction between "forced" and "voluntary" prostitution. (The former term refers to the key role of coercion, violence, and intimidation by third parties while the latter refers to the free choice of occupation.) Groups working on behalf of sex workers worry that the concern with trafficking, with its emphasis on forced prostitution, will impede the campaign for the rights and dignity of all sex workers, the vast majority of whom are not trafficked. Jo Doezema (1998), for one, worries that the focus on young and innocent victims in so many reports on trafficking implies that women who choose prostitution are worthy of contempt rather than respect. Critics of the dichotomy also point out that anti-trafficking efforts based on faulty premises—that the women are always duped, that they are total victims—are bound to founder.

56. Brussa 1998.

6

~~

Beyond Sicily

In the course of this book we have endeavored to describe the life and times of recent immigrants to Sicily. The focus on three forms of dirty work—domestic service, farm labor, and prostitution—reflects our assessment of the very limited opportunities awaiting foreigners on this Mediterranean island. True, the immigrant population has increased over time and the number of countries represented continues to lengthen. Immigrants operate restaurants and shops, they organize and frequent temples, mosques, and other places of worship, they form associations. Newcomers gather in Sicilian squares and join unions and civic groups. Growing numbers have decided to enroll their children in Sicilian schools and in some areas we find a second generation more at home in Italy than in Tunisia or Mauritius. Despite the evident diversity and undeniable accomplishments of immigrants and their children, their economic role and political status in Sicilian life has changed little since the arrival thirty years ago of farm workers from Tunisia and maids from the Philippines. Today, as in the past, few escape low-status, dead-end, and poorly paid employment. Needing to support themselves and their families back home, possessing few marketable skills in a tightly contested labor market, and in many cases lacking documentation, immigrants are compelled to accept the dirty work that Sicilians refuse.

As distinctive as the sectors described in this book are, they all do similar things to newcomers. In each we see the relegation of foreign workers to the bottom of a segmented labor market and the margins of society, the development of ethnic and racial stereotypes and identities within the crucible of the labor market, the cultivation of networks both enabling and limiting, and the costs and benefits experienced by transnational families. We have also noted the simultaneous dependence on and anxiety over foreign workers among Sicilians. Sicily, with its history of emigration, has long received goods and ideas from abroad. Only in the past twenty years have Sicilians come to depend on foreign laborers living in the midst. The irony that Africans, Asians, and others now perform degrading jobs as Sicilians once did in New York, Buenos Aires, Sydney, and Turin is not lost on Sicilians. As we have seen, they react to this unexpected reversal with wonder and pride, empathy and self-interest.

The three cases also demonstrate that hardship, even danger, serve as constant companions to immigrants in Sicily. Domestic workers, particularly those who live with their employers, must reside apart from their families and delay or forego creating a family of their own. As their stories suggest, lack of respect, underpayment, and sexual harassment figure among the occupational hazards of residing with one's employer. Tunisian men toil long hours for little, are exposed to a veritable arsenal of chemicals in greenhouses, and are dismissed as soon as their labor is no longer needed or profitable. For the Nigerian prostitutes, serving Sicilian clients entails daily humiliation and carries the constant threat of disease, theft, and violence. Subservience to traffickers entails a many-sided exploitation and involves emotional and quite possibly physical violence.

In all three sectors we register an unacknowledged subsidy of sorts in which high personal costs in one part of the world underwrite prodigious consumption in another. The costs are often borne by transnational households, families whose members remain linked by exchanges of information, emotional support, and money even as they remain separated by thousands of miles. Husbands and wives relocate half a world away to support their families while parents may diversify their assets by sending grown sons and daughters abroad. This involves a transfer of resources from poorer to richer areas because the costs of raising, training, and caring for workers are unevenly distributed. As we have seen, adult men and women of diverse origins arrive ready to accept employment caring for Sicilians and their households. To assist their own families, these wandering caregivers and cleaners must be ready to endure long-term physical separation from the homes and homelands that nourished them. Tunisian men at the peak of their physical powers work in Vittoria and Santa Croce most of the year, costing the Italian state little and conferring savings on Sicilian farmers and on consumers throughout Europe. Meanwhile, the Tunisian state and society, particularly the men's wives and mothers and cousins, rear the next generation at home. Some Nigerian women take the calculated risk of entering sex work in Europe in order to support children back home, while others may hope that their earnings in

Turin or Palermo will aid their parents in Benin City. Even a brief career as a sex worker in Europe, which could easily involve disease and physical and emotional trauma, translates into high costs for the returning women and their families and localities in Nigeria. Michael Blim has argued that the participation of more people in more places in capitalist relations has increased rather than decreased inequality globally.[1] Our survey appears to confirm this assessment.

Barring the unlikely collapse of the region's economy, immigration to Sicily will continue for the foreseeable future. The networks linking established immigrant populations to friends, family, and communities abroad, and the thriving business in the licit and illicit movement of people across international borders ensure an almost limitless supply of new arrivals. Pressures felt by Sicilian families and businesses, coupled with a preference for the flexibility of informal arrangements, all but guarantee the continued reliance on foreign labor, at least in the lower levels of the opportunity structure. For their part, Sicilian men continue to demonstrate a demand, albeit less than their northern peers, for the services of foreign street prostitutes. The more foreigners perform dirty work, the less palatable it becomes to Sicilian youth and their families. Even as Sicilian families and farms have come to depend on immigrants, they regard the growth of a distinct and marginalized population within their midst with concern if not alarm. In the depressingly familiar logic of stratified societies, those who perform dirty work are regarded as dirty rather than clean, as charity cases rather than as contributors.

Just as inevitable as continued immigration is immigrant mobility. An immigrant's first years are very demanding. The initial flush of excitement at having arrived in Europe is followed by disillusionment. The work is arduous and possibly dangerous, the wages low and the costs of living high, the hosts by turns demanding, uncaring, sympathetic. With time, the immigrant learns to communicate in Italian, develops marketable skills, and comes to appreciate the prospects for a better life. But discrimination, competition from Sicilians, and circumscribed social networks tend to limit chances for stable employment if not advancement. Individual success stories aside, the choice for most immigrants is to accept dirty work and struggle against great odds to achieve recognition and stable employment, or to leave for the Italian center-north or another country. Because so many opt to depart, immigration to Sicily is more a process through which individuals and families flow than a set of discrete and stable communities of foreign origins. As a Ghanaian man expressed it, Sicily is a transit zone and a stay in Palermo resembles an extended delay at the gate of an airport terminal. Immigrant movement within a destination country is not uncommon. What is distinctive about the Sicilian case today, and quite possibly about the southern

European case in general, is the degree to which upward mobility is limited. To move up, one must literally move on and even then the ascent is strewn with obstacles.

In the Italian context, the factories, industrial farms, and service sectors of the north promise stable employment and draw many immigrants from Sicily and other southern areas. The northward path of foreigners today bears a striking resemblance to the exodus of Sicilian peasants from the late nineteenth century through the 1970s. Political oppression, the stifling presence of organized crime, grinding poverty, and relegation to dirty work prompted many Sicilians to leave home, while active recruitment and social networks facilitated their integration into northern labor markets. For local elites, the mass departures promised an influx of remittances and served to dampen the uprisings and calls for economic justice to which peasants and their advocates had periodically given vent. After World War II, the ruling Christian Democrats (DC) forsook a strategy of economic development in favor of honing a patronage system in which they doled out state resources in return for electoral support. Members of a rising middle class secured a stable perch in an economy driven by government spending and services. In a context of high unemployment and limited opportunities, many Sicilians took their skills elsewhere; the outbound movement reached a peak in the 1960s and 1970s but continues today, particularly among the young and educated.

For immigrants, the prevalence of undocumented employment and the casual attitude toward controls make Sicily attractive. Indeed, like Augustine, many immigrants grow quite fond of Sicily and Sicilians. But like the peasants of old, today's newcomers have little hope of improving their situation on the island and so have sought economic stability and social mobility through relocation. Unlike peasants, immigrants have fewer affective ties and supports on the island. Many see their sojourn in Sicily as but one leg in an ongoing migratory project, so they do not hesitate to leave when better opportunities present themselves elsewhere. Like Sicilian peasants before them, immigrants today represent a pool of labor power ready to fuel the economic turbines of the north. During their time in Sicily newcomers learn the language, become familiar with Italian ways, and gain work experience; by the time they obtain a permit, they are prepared to journey north. In this sense Sicily's historic role as a labor reservoir for northern capitalists has simply taken on an international aspect with immigrant mobility.

What are future prospects for immigrants in Sicily? In their review of contemporary global population movement, Stephen Castles and Mark Miller conclude that in the long run the incorporation of foreigners results in the development of "ethnic minorities" and "ethnic communities." The former condition obtains when a settled immigrant population lives at the margins of society and is seen as undesirable, their rights limited, their contributions unacknowledged. In the later scenario, communities of immigrant origin are viewed as legitimate and contributing members of a multicultural society. As Castles and Miller note, most situations fall between these poles.[2]

Immigration to Sicily is of recent origins and so the arc of ethnicity has yet to reveal its course. A consideration of the current state of affairs does not however give much cause for optimism. True, elements of Italian government (and European Union) policy favor integration, recognize cultural diversity, and reject discrimination and racism. The centrality of emigration to recent Italian history and a fragmented sense of national identity may allow symbolic space for newcomers in an evolving Italian identity. On the other hand, a casual attitude toward entries (especially early on) and lax enforcement of labor laws have nurtured a large foreign population vulnerable to exploitation by virtue of precarious economic and legal status. Repeated amnesties have offered temporary legal status to hundreds of thousands, but few foreigners have gained the security of the valued permanent permit and even fewer have naturalized. Indeed, children born in Italy to foreign parents are considered foreign nationals until the age of 18 and even then are eligible for citizenship only if a series of conditions are met. The 2002 immigration law, the product of a Center-Right coalition government, ties the right to continued residence more tightly than ever to proof of employment, and reflects a view of immigrants as disposable workers. The idea of sending foreign workers home when they are no longer needed certainly appeals to an economic model of population movement. In fact governments in other countries have also justified amnesties and recruitment programs as temporary measures. But as case after case has demonstrated, workers are people not merely labor; immigration flows, once initiated and encouraged, continue by force of social networks and labor demand. The denial of these realities is a perilous basis for government policy and practice and only contributes to the undesirable formation of disadvantaged minorities.

Lax enforcement has made Palermo and Sicily in general a destination of choice for those lacking permits, but the same inefficiency has produced few measures promoting integration. Owing to widespread employer preference for informal arrangements, undocumented immigrants can easily find dirty work in Sicily while those with permits or higher aspirations encounter more problems and are often compelled to leave the island in search of upward mobility. Immigrants who have left Sicily for the north favorably contrast the sociable character of Sicilians with the closed attitudes of their new northern neighbors and bosses. Sicilians are wont to criticize the northern Italian communities and parties that have mobilized politically against immigrants. Yet many Sicilians have not hesitated to depict the dark-skinned foreigners from Asia and African in their midst as distinct, different, and ill-equipped to make meaningful contributions to Sicilian society. These circumstances do not bode well for the development of vibrant ethnic communities.

If the development of a middle class of African or Asian origins appears unlikely in Sicily, it is by no means assured elsewhere in Italy. Areas of the center-north, among the richest and most productive in all of Europe, have recently exhibited an insatiable appetite for foreign labor. As we have noted, many immigrants have left Palermo to don the worker's blue uniform in factories, foundries, and industrial farms. While a variety of views with regard to immigrants find expression among Italians north of Rome, perhaps the loudest and most insistent voice is that of the Northern League. The party, which rose to national prominence in the 1990s and has been a member of two recent governing coalitions, has called for fiscal reform and the independence of localities from the central government. It co-sponsored the 2002 immigration legislation. In the League's estimation, immigrants serve a useful purpose as temporary, permit-bearing, and tax-paying workers; too distant culturally to assimilate into Italian society, they should be encouraged to go home as soon as their labor is no longer needed.

Immigrants who have relocated from Palermo to the far north judge the League's position a cynical attempt to gain electoral support among those who benefit most from the immigrant workforce. While they are relieved to have found steady jobs, benefits, and the legal status such employment grants, immigrants complain that the good jobs always seem to go to Italians and that locals wish to limit interactions to the workplace. Our field research has taken us to a single small northern industrial center where we encountered some two-dozen Ivorians formerly resident in Palermo. Our admittedly impressionistic data, however, appears to find corroboration in general studies that revealed widespread workplace discrimination in Italian industrial settings.[3] Children of immigrant parents who have grown up in (northern) Italy report a pattern of unpleasant experiences in shops, with police, and at work; they observe that they are defined as foreign nationals in the country of their birth. Taken together, these points make the second generation feel as though they will never be regarded as properly belonging in Italy.[4] If these reports are accurate, Italy risks an unsettling future in which a permanent minority population of foreign origins experiences social exclusion. This scenario is likely to take strongest hold in the center-north, owing to the northward pull we have described and the hostile tenor of some influential and outspoken elements of northern society. The short-term mentality—temporary permits and dirty work for desperate foreigners—so characteristic of recent Italian policy is a blueprint for long-term trouble. Because the recent transition to immigrant destination has been handled in similar ways across southern Europe, the meaningful incorporation of newcomers and their children appears unlikely from Portugal to Greece. The unsettling integration of immigrant communities, especially Muslim ones, in northwestern Europe has captured much media attention of late. Trends in Italy suggest that immigration may become a flash point across the southern border of the European Union as well.

The lives of foreign farm workers, domestics, and prostitutes in Sicily should also alert us to trends in our society. Of course, immigration stands at the core of national identity in the United States and the arrival of diverse peoples is synonymous with the country's history. For foreigners, the path to citizenship is celebrated and millions of new citizens express pride in their adopted homeland. In a context of opportunities and constraints, immigrants and their children are incorporated into United States society in every way, from the undocumented farm hand to the billionaire financier. And yet there is no denying that here as in Sicily newcomers perform most of the dirtiest jobs. Here too a combination of feeble enforcement of labor laws, legal restrictions on entry, and porous borders permit the employment and exploitation of foreign workers made vulnerable by undocumented status and economic need. And here too, despite a range of views, many native born express anxiety over the growing immigrant population and the associated costs while they simultaneously deny or minimize the contributions of immigrants and their families. While there is more to immigration than dirty work, there appears to be little dirty work that does not involve immigrants. This labor is tough, demeaning, even dangerous, and it is performed by the most vulnerable among us. The Sicilian case should prompt us to question the causes and consequences of the work we cannot live without and would all prefer to avoid.

NOTES

1. Blim 2005.
2. Castles and Miller 1998.
3. See, e.g., Reyneri 2004b.
4. Andall 2002.

Bibliography

3A. 2002. www.dsonline.it/aree/agricoltura/documenti (accessed, April 15, 2002).

Abbatecola, Emanuela. 2002. "Le reti insidiose: Organizzazione e percorsi della tratta fra coercizione e produzione del 'consenso.'" Pp. 69–133 in *Comprate e vendute: Una ricerca su tratta e sfruttamento di donne straniere nel mercato della prostituzione*, ed. Maurizio Ambrosini. Milan: FrancoAngeli.

Agosta, Ida, and Stefania Chironi. 2000. "L'immigrazione nordafricana in Italia: Il rapporto con l'agricoltura della Sicilia." Paper presented at XVIèmes Rencontres de l'ARTHUSE, les relations entre les pays de l'Union Européenne et les pays du Bassin de la Méditerranée, Seville, Spain.

Aiello, Francesco. 1987. "Momenti ed aspetti della serricoltura: l'esperienza del Ragusano." Pp. 154–64 in *Cinquant'anni di agricoltura in Sicilia dagli anni '30 agli anni '80: Atti del Convegno Regionale*. Ragusa: Centro Studi Feliciano Rossitto.

Albano, Teresa. 2002. "IOM Rome Takes 'Systematic Action' on Article 18 of Italy's Aliens Law." *Trafficking in Migrants* 26: 6. Geneva: International Organization for Migration.

Ambrosini, Maurizio. 2001. *La fatica di integrarsi*. Bologna: Il Mulino.

———, ed. 2002. *Comprate e vendute: Una ricerca su tratta e sfruttamento di donne straniere nel mercato della prostituzione*. Milan: FrancoAngeli.

Andall, Jacqueline. 1998. "Catholic and State Constructions of Domestic Workers: The Case of Cape Verdean Women in Rome in the 1970s." Pp. 124–42 in *The New Migration in Europe: Social Constructions and Social Realities*, ed. Khalid Koser and Helma Lutz. London: Macmillian.

———. 1999. "Cape Verdean Women on the Move." *Modern Italy* 4, no. 2: 241–57.

———. 2000a. *Gender, Migration and Domestic Service: The Politics of Black Women in Italy.* Aldershot: Ashgate.

———. 2000b. "Organizing Domestic Workers in Italy: The Challenge of Gender, Class and Ethnicity." Pp. 145–71 in *Gender and Migration in Southern Europe: Women on the Move,* ed. Floya Anthias and Gabriella Lazaridis. Oxford and New York: Berg.

———. 2002. "Second-Generation Attitude? African-Italians in Milan." *Journal of Ethnic and Migration Studies* 28, no. 3: 389–407.

———, ed. 2003. *Gender and Ethnicity in Contemporary Europe.* Oxford and New York: Berg.

Andall, Jacqueline, and Russell King. 1999. The Geography and Economic Sociology of Recent Immigration to Italy. *Modern Italy* 4, no. 2: 135–58.

Anderson, Bridget. 2000. *Doing the Dirty Work: The Global Politics of Domestic Labor.* London and New York: Zed Books.

Anthias, Floya, and Gabriella Lazaridis, eds. 2000. *Gender and Migration in Southern Europe: Women on the Move.* Oxford and New York: Berg.

Asowa-Omorodion, Francisca. 2000. "Sexual and Health Behavior of Commercial Sex Workers in Benin City, Edo State, Nigeria." *Health Care for Women International* 21: 335–45.

Bacci, Massimo Livi. 2000. "The Question of Immigration." *Review of Economic Conditions in Italy* 2–3: 221–43.

Balibar, Etienne. 1991. "Is there a 'Neo-Racism'?" Pp. 17–28 in *Race, Nation, Class: Ambiguous Identities,* ed. Etienne Balibar and Immanuel Wallerstein. New York: Verso Press.

Bamgbose, Oluyemesi. 2002. "Teenage Prostitution and the Future of the Female Adolescent in Nigeria." *International Journal of Offender Therapy and Comparative Criminology* 46, no. 5: 569–85.

Bellassai, Emanuele, and Bartolo Scillieri. 2000. "Immigrazione e internazionalizzazione nelle provincia di Ragusa." Pp. 65–80 in *Immigrazione e processi di internazionalizzazione dei sistemi produttivi italiani,* ed. CeSPI (Centro Studi di Politica Internazionale). Presidenza del Consiglio dei Ministri, Working Paper No. 9. Roma: Dipartimento per gli affairi sociali.

Blim, Michael. 2005. *Equality and Economy: The Global Challenge.* Lanham, MD: Altamira Press.

Bonifazi, Corrado. 2000. "European Migration Policy: Questions from Italy." Pp. 233–52 in *Eldorado or Fortress? Migration in Southern Europe,* ed. Russell King, Gabriella Lazaridis, and Charalambos Tsardanidis. London: Macmillan.

Booth, Sally. 1997. "Changing Geographies of Class and Gender: Earthquake Reconstruction in Western Sicily." Ph.D. diss., Graduate School of the City University of New York.

———. 1999. "Changing Patterns of Sexual Geography in Western Sicilian New Towns." Pp. 133–56 in *House Life: Space, Place, and Family in Europe,* ed. Donna Birdwell-Pheasant and Denise Lawrence-Zuniga. Berg: Oxford.

Booth, Sally, and Jeffrey Cole. 1999. "An Unsettling Integration: Immigrant Lives and Work in Palermo." *Modern Italy* 4, no. 2: 191–205.

Boven, Frank, Dina Siegel, and Damián Zaitich. 2003. "Organized Crime and Ethnic Reputation Manipulation." *Crime, Law & Social Change* 39: 23–38.

Brettell, Caroline. 1995. *We Have Already Cried Many Tears: The Stories of Three Portuguese Migrant Women*. Prospect Heights, IL: Waveland Press.

———. 2003. "Migration Stories: Agency and the Individual in the Study of Migration." Pp. 23–45 in *Anthropology and Migration: Essays on Transnationalism, Ethnicity, and Identity*. Walnut Creek, CA: Altamira Press.

Brettell, Caroline, and James Hollifield, eds. 2000. *Migration Theory*. New York and London: Routledge.

Brussa, Licia. 1998. "The Tampep Project in Western Europe." Pp. 246–59 in *Global Sex Workers*, ed. Kemala Kempadoo and Jo Doezema. Routledge: New York and London.

Buzzi, Carlo. 1998. *Giovani, Affettività, Sessualità*. Il Mulino: Bologna.

Campani, Giovanna. 2000. "Immigrant Women in Southern Europe: Social Exclusion, Domestic Work and Prostitution in Italy." Pp. 145–69 in *Eldorado or Fortress? Migration in Southern Europe*, ed. Russell King, Gabriella Lazaridis, and Charalambos Tsardanidis. London: Macmillan.

———. 2001. "Migrants and the Media: The Italian Case." Pp. 38–52 in *Media and Migration*, ed. Russell King and Nancy Wood. New York and London: Routledge.

Carbonin, Pier Ugo, Roberto Bernabei, Giuseppe Zuccalà, and Giovanni Gambassi. 1997. "Health-care for Older persons, a Country Profile: Italy." *Journal of the American Geriatrics Society* 45, no. 12: 1519–22.

Carchedi, Francesco, Anna Picciolini, Giovanni Mottura, and Giovanna Campani. 2000. *I colori della notte*. Milan: FrancoAngeli.

Caritas di Roma. 1997. *Immigrazione: Dossier statistico 1997*. Rome: Anterem.

———. 2000. *Immigrazione: Dossier statistico 2002*. Rome: Anterem.

———. 2001. *Immigrazione: Dossier statistico 2001*. Rome: Anterem.

———. 2002. *Immigrazione: Dossier statistico 2002*. Rome: Anterem.

———. 2003. *Immigrazione: Dossier statistico 2003*. Rome: Anterem.

Caritas Diocesana Ragusa. 1994. *Dal terzo mondo in Italia: L'immigrazione in provincia di Ragusa: Dossier 1994*. Ragusa: Caritas Diocesana Ragusa.

Castles, Stephen, and Godula Kosack. 1985. *Immigrant Workers and Class Structure in Western Europe*. 2nd ed. London: Oxford University Press.

Castles, Stephen, and Mark Miller. 1998. *The Age of Migration: International Population Movements in the Modern World*. 2nd ed. New York and London: Guilford Press.

CENSIS (Centro Studi Investimenti Sociali). 2000. "I comportamenti sessuali degli italiani. Rome: CENSIS." www.censis.it/censis/ricerche/2000/i_comportamenti_sessuali_degli_i.htm (accessed February 5, 2003).

Chell, Victoria. 2000. "Female Migrants in Italy: Coping in a Country of New Migration." Pp. 103–23 in *Gender and Migration in Southern Europe: Women on the Move*, ed. Floya Anthias and Gabriella Lazaridis. Oxford and New York: Berg.

Christian, William Jr. 2000. "Eunice and Edgar: The International Traffic in Care." Pp. 119–22 in *Miniature ethnografiche*, ed. Henk Driessen and Huub de Jonge. Nijmegen: SUN.

Chubb, Judith. 1982. *Patronage, Power and Poverty: A Tale of Two Cities.* Cambridge: Cambridge University Press.

CIHEAM (International Centre for Advanced Mediterranean Agronomic Studies). 2000. *Annual Report 2000: Development and agri-food policies in the Mediterranean region.* Paris: CIHEAM.

Cirivello, Teresa. 2001. "L'impiego degli immigrati extracomunitari nel settore dell'agricoltura in Sicilia nel 2001." Unpublished annual report conducted for the Istituto Nazionale di Economia Agraria (INEA).

Cole, Jeffrey. 1997. *The New Racism in Europe: A Sicilian Ethnography.* Cambridge: Cambridge University Press.

———. 2003. "Borders Past and Present in Mazara del Vallo, Sicily." *European Studies* 19: 195–216.

Collinson, Sarah. 1996. *Shore to Shore: The Politics of Migration in Euro-Maghreb Relations.* London: The Royal Institute of International Affairs.

Colombo, Enzo. 1999a. "I clienti della prostituzione: una possibile tipologia." Pp. 39–63 in *Sesso in acquisto: Una ricerca sui clienti della prostituzione,* ed. Luisa Leonini. Milan: Edizioni Unicopli.

———. 1999b. "Alcune possibili interpretazioni della relazione cliente-prostituta." Pp. 147–58 in *Sesso in acquisto: Una ricerca sui clienti della prostituzione,* ed. Luisa Leonini. Milan: Edizioni Unicopli.

Covre, Pia with Rosanna Paradiso. 2000. "Southern Region Report." European Network for HIV/STD Prevention in Prostitution. www.europap.net/regional/southern.regional.htm (accessed October 24, 2002).

Cusumano, Antonio. 1976. *Il ritorno infelice.* Palermo: Sellerio.

———. 2000. *Cittadini senza cittidinanza: Rapporto duemila sulla presenza degli stranieri a Mazara del Vallo.* Gibellina: CRESM.

Dale, Gareth, and Mike Cole, eds. 1999. *The European Union and Migrant Labour.* Oxford and New York: Berg.

Daly, Faïçal. 2001. The Double Passage: Tunisian Migration to the South and North of Italy. Pp. 186–205 in *The Mediterranean Passage,* ed. Russell King. Liverpool: Liverpool University Press.

DaMolin, Giovanna. 1990. "Family Forms and Domestic Service in Southern Italy." *Journal of Family History* 15, no. 4: 503–27.

Dell'Orto, Federica, and Patrizia Taccani. 1993. "Family Carers and Dependent Elderly People in Italy." Pp. 109–28 in *Informal Care in Europe,* ed. Julia Twigg. York: Social Policy Research Unit, University of York.

Di Cortemiglia, Vittoria Luda. 2003. "Programme of Action against Trafficking in Minors and Young Women from Nigeria to Italy for the Purpose of Sexual Exploitation." Desk Review. Turin: UNICRI (United Nations Interregional Crime and Justice Research Institute).

DIA (Direzione Investigativa Antimafia). 2000. *Attività Svolta e Risultati Conseguiti*. Rome: Ministero dell'Interno. Anno 2000-2° Semestre. Rome: Ministero dell' Interno.

———. 2003a. *La Direzionze Investigativa Antimafia e l'azione di contrasto alla criminalità organizzata di tipo mafioso*. Anno 2003-2° Semestre, Vol. 1. Rome: Ministero dell'Interno.

———. 2003b. *Attività di analisi, progettualità e strategia operativa della Direzione Investigativa Antimafia*. Anno 2003-2° Semestre, Vol. 2. Rome: Ministero dell' Interno.

Doezema, Jo. 1998. "Forced to Choose: Beyond the Voluntary v. Forced Prostitution Dichotomy." Pp. 34–50 in *Global Sex Workers*, ed. Kamala Kempadoo and Jo Doezema. New York and London: Routledge.

Extra. 1998. Preliminary Research Report, Progetto LIA. Palermo: Author.

Fakiolas, Rossetos. 2000. "Migration and Unregistered Labour in the Greek Economy." Pp. 57–78 in *Eldorado or Fortress? Migration in Southern Europe*, ed. Russell King, Gabriella Lazaridis, and Charalambos Tsardanidis. London: Macmillan.

Favaro, Grazilella. 1993. "Avere un figlio altrove." Pp. 141–53 in *Le mani invisibili: la vita e il lavoro delle donne immigrate*, ed. Giovanna Vicarelli. Rome: Ediesse.

GEOPA (General Committee for Agricultural Cooperation in the European Union). 2002. "Seasonal Workers in European Agriculture." Brussels: COPA (Committee of Agricultural Organisations in the European Union).

Giavatto, Giuseppe. 2001. "Sviluppare l'agroindustria, migliorare qualità e competitività dei prodotti, tutelare i consumatori, difendere e garantire i diritti dei lavoratori." Relazione introduttiva, congresso provinciale della Flai-Cgil. Conference presentation, November 23, Kastalia.

Gibson, Mary. 1993. "Italy." Pp. 157–76 in *Prostitution: An International Handbook of Trends, Problems, and Policies*, ed. Nanette Davis. Westport, CT: Greenwood Press.

———. 1999. *Prostitution and the State in Italy, 1860–1915*. 2nd ed. Columbus, OH: Ohio State University Press.

Griffith, David, and Ed Kissam. 1995. *Working Poor: Farmworkers in the U.S.* Philadelphia, PA: Temple University Press.

Grillo, Ralph, and Jeff Pratt, eds. 2002. *The Politics of Recognizing Difference: Multiculturalism Italian Style*. Aldershot: Ashgate.

Gülçür, Leyla, and Pinar İlkkaracan. 2002. "The 'Natasha' Experience: Migrant Sex Workers from the Former Soviet Union and Eastern Europe in Turkey." *Women's Studies International Forum* 25, no. 4: 411–21.

Hannachi, Karim. 1998. *Gli immigrati tunsini a Mazara del Vallo*. Gibellina: CRESM.

Heyman, Josiah McC. 2002. "U.S. Immigration Officers of Mexican Ancestry as Mexican Americans, Citizens, and Immigration Police." *Current Anthropology* 43, no. 3: 479–507.

Hoggart, Keith, and Cristóbal Mendoza. 1999. "African Immigrant Workers in Spanish Agriculture." *Sociologia Ruralis* 39, no. 4: 538–62.

Holmes-Eber, Paula. 2003. *Daughters of Tunis: Women, Family, and Networks in a Muslim City.* Boulder, CO: Westview Press.

Hondagneu-Sotelo, Pierrette. 2001. *Doméstica: Immigrant Workers Cleaning and Caring in the Shadows of Affluence.* Berkeley, CA: University of California Press.

ICMPD (International Centre for Migration Policy Development). 1999. "The Relationship between Organised Crime and Trafficking in Aliens." Study prepared by the Secretariat of the Budapest Group. ICMPD: Vienna.

INEA (Istituto Nazionale di Economia Agraria). 1998. "Italian Agriculture 1998." Rome: INEA.

———. 1999. "Italian Agriculture 1999." Rome: INEA.

Iori, Luca, and Giovanni Mottura. 1989. "Stranieri in agricoltura: Cenni su un aspetto della struttura dell'occupazione agricola in Italia." Pp. 581–90 in *Stranieri in Italia,* ed. Giovanni Cocchi. Bologna: Il Mulino.

Istituto Nazionale di Statistica (ISTAT). 2006. "Territorial Indicators." sistis.istat.it/sistis./html/index.htm (accessed July 24, 2006).

Jiménez-Díaz, José. 2003. "The Process of Globalization in an Andalusian Town: Study of 'El Ejido.'" Pp. 95–112 in *Local Reactions to Globalization,* ed. Francesco Entrena. New York: Nova Science Publications.

Justice and Home Affairs, European Community. 2001. "Trafficking in Women." www.europa.eu.int/comm/justice_home/news/8mars.en.htm (accessed December 2, 2002).

Kempadoo, Kamala. 1998. "Introduction." Pp. 1–28 in *Global Sex Workers,* ed. Kamala Kempadoo and Jo Doezema. New York and London: Routledge.

———, ed. 1999. *Sun, Sex and Gold: Tourism and Sex Work in the Caribbean.* New York: Rowan & Littlefield.

Kempadoo, Kamala, and Jo Doezema, eds. 1998. *Global Sex Workers.* New York and London: Routledge.

King, Russell. 2000. "Southern Europe in the Changing Global Map of Migration." Pp. 1–26 in *Eldorado or Fortress? Migration in Southern Europe,* ed. Russell King, Gabriella Lazaridis, and Charalambos Tsardanidis. London: Macmillan.

King, Russell, and Natalia Ribas-Mateos. 2002. "Toward a Diversity of Migratory Types and Contexts in Southern Europe." *Studi Emigrazione* 39: 5–26.

King, Russell, Tony Warnes, and Allan Williams. 2000. *Sunset Lives: British Retirement Migration to the Mediterranean.* Oxford and New York: Berg.

Lamphere, Louise. 1987. *From Working Daughters to Working Mothers: Immigrant Women in a New England Industrial Community.* Ithaca, NY: Cornell University Press.

———, ed. 1992. *Structuring Diversity: Ethnographic Perspectives on the New Immigration.* Chicago: University of Chicago Press.

Lamphere, Lousie, Alex Stepick, and Guillermo Grenier, eds. 1994. *Newcomers to the Workplace: Immigrants and the Restructuring of the U.S. Economy.* Philadelphia: Temple University Press.

Lazaridis, Gabriella. 2000. "Filipino and Albanian Women Migrant Workers in Greece: Multiple Layers of Oppression." Pp. 15–47 in *Gender and Migration in*

Southern Europe: Women on the Move, ed. Floya Anthias and Gabriella Lazaridis. Oxford and New York: Berg.

Leonini, Luisa. 1999a. "La ricerca sui clienti." Pp. 11–37 in *Sesso in acquisto: Una ricerca sui clienti della prostituzione*, ed. Lusia Leonini. Milan: Edizioni Unicopli.

——, ed. 1999. *Sesso in acquisto: Una ricerca sui clienti della prostituzione*. Milan: Edizioni Unicopli.

Lever, Janet, and Deanne Dolnick. 2000. "Clients and Call Girls: Seeking Sex and Intimacy." Pp. 85–100 in *Sex for Sale: Prostitution, Pornography, and the Sex Industry*, ed. Ronald Weitzer. New York and London: Routledge.

Lombezzi, Mimmo. 1998. "La strada di Olga." *D, La Repubblica delle donne* 3/111: 14–18.

Lucassen, Jan, and Leo Lucassen. 1997. "Migration, Migration History, History." Pp. 9–38 in *Migration, Migration History, History: Old Paradigms and New Perspectives*, ed. Jan Lucassen and Leo Lucassen. Berne: Peter Lang.

Maluccelli, Lorenza. 2002. "Da prostitute a domestiche: Storie di mercati 'sommersi' e donne 'in transizione.'" Pp. 225–54 in *Stranieri in Italia: Assimilati ed esclusi*, ed. Asher Colombo and Giuseppe Sciortino. Bologna: Il Mulino.

Massey, Douglas, Joaquim Arango, Graeme Hugo, Ali Kouaouci, Adela Pellegrino, and J. Edward Taylor. 1998. *Worlds in Motion: Understanding International Migration at the End of the Millennium*. Oxford: Clarendon Press.

Meli, Angelo. 1998. "Come inventarsi un lavoro." *Il Quartiere Nuovo* 4, no. 2: 10–11.

Mestheneos, Elizabeth, and Judith Triantafillou. 1993. "Dependent Elderly People in Greece and Their Family Carers." Pp. 129–50 in *Informal Care in Europe*, ed. Julia Twigg. York: Social Policy Research Unit, University of York.

Miccichè, Giuseppe. 1987. "Le campagne siciliane tra gli anni '30 e gli anni '40." Pp. 86–97 in *Cinquant'anni di agricoltura in Sicilia dagli anni '30 agli anni '80: Atti del Convegno Regionale*. Ragusa: Centro Studi Feliciano Rossitto.

——. 1997. "Sindacato e lotte dei lavoratori nei comuni iblei." *Annali* 6: 5–45. Ragusa: Centro Studi Feliciano Rossitto.

——. 2000. *Il difficile sviluppo: Sindacati e lotte del lavoro nei comuni iblei dale origini ad oggi*. Ragusa: Centro Studi Felciano Rossitto.

Mingione, Enzo, and Fabio Quassoli. 2000. "The Participation of Immigrants in the Underground Economy in Italy." Pp. 27–56 in *Eldorado or Fortress? Migration in Southern Europe*, ed. Russell King, Gabriella Lazaridis, and Charalambos Tsardanidis. London: Macmillan.

Monto, Martin. 2000. "Why Men Seek Out Prostitutes." Pp. 67–83 in *Sex for Sale: Prostitution, Pornography, and the Sex Industry*, ed. Ronald Weitzer. New York and London: Routledge.

O'Connell Davidson, Julia. 1998. *Prostitution, Power and Freedom*. Ann Arbor: University of Michigan Press.

O'Connell Davidson, Julia, and Jacqueline Sanchez Taylor. 1999. "Fantasy Islands: Exploring the Demand for Sex Tourism." Pp. 37–54 in *Sun, Sex and Gold*, ed. Kamala Kempadoo. New York: Rowman & Littlefield.

Okojie, Christiana. 2003. *Programme of Action Against Trafficking in Minors and Young Women from Nigeria to Italy for the Purpose of Sexual Exploitation: Report of Field Survey in Edo State, Nigeria.* Turin: United Nations Interregional Crime and Justice Research Unit (UNICRI).

Okonfua, F., S. Ogbomwan, A. Alutu, O. Kufre, and A. Eghosa. 2004. "Knowledge, Attitudes and Experiences of Sex Trafficking by Young Women in Benin City, South-South Nigeria." *Social Science and Medicine* 59: 1315–27.

Omorodion, Francisca. 1993. "Sexual Networking among Market Women in Benin City, Benin State, Nigeria." *Health Transition Review* 3 (supplementary issue): 1–11.

O'Neill, Maggie, and Rosemary Barberet. 2000. "Victimization and the Social Organization of Prostitution." In *Sex for Sale: Prostitution, Pornography, and the Sex Industry,* ed. Ronald Weitzer, 123–37. New York and London: Routledge.

Ortiz, Sutti. 2002. "Laboring in the Factories and the Fields." *Annual Review of Anthropology* 31: 395–417.

OSCE (Organisation for Security and Co-operation in Europe). 1999. *Trafficking in Human Beings: Implications for the OSCE.* Background Paper 1993/3. Vienna: OSCE. www.osce.org/odihr/documents/background/trafficking/ (accessed December 2, 2002).

Population Division of the Department of Economic and Social Affairs of the United Nations. 2006. "World Migrant Stock: The 2005 Revision Population Database." esa.un.org/migration/p2k0data.asp (accessed July 10, 2006).

Portes, Alejandro, and Rubén Rumbaut. 2001a. *Legacies: The Story of the Immigrant Second Generation.* Berkeley: University of California Press.

———, eds. 2001b. *Ethnicities: Children of Immigrants in America.* Berkeley: University of California Press.

———. 1996. *Immigrant America: A Portrait.* 2nd ed. Berkeley: University of California Press.

Prina, Francesco. 2003. *Action Programme Against the Traffic from Nigeria to Italy of Minors and Young Women for Sexual Exploitation. Trade and Exploitation of Minors and Young Nigerian Women for Prostitution in Italy.* Research Report, July 2003. Turin: United Nations Interregional Crime and Justice Research Unit (UNICRI).

Pugliese, Enrico. 1991. "L'immigrazione in agricoltura: Il caso di Villa Literno." Pp. 176–82 in *La presenza straniera in Italia: Il caso della Campania,* ed. Francesco Calvanese and Enrico Pugliese. Milan: FrancoAngeli.

———. 1993. "Restructuring of the Labour Market and the Role of Third World Migrations in Europe." *Society and Space* 11: 513–22.

———. 1998 [1991]. "Gli immigrati nel mercato del lavoro e nella economia italiana." Pp. 50–71 in *Gli immigrati in Italia,* ed. Maria Macioti and Enrico Pulgiese. Rome and Bari: Laterza.

Renda, Francesco. 1989 [1963]. *L'emigrazione in Sicilia, 1652–1961.* Aggiornamento di Eugenio Greco. Caltanisetta and Rome: Salvatore Sciascia Editore.

Reyneri, Emilio. 1998. "The Role of the Underground Economy in Irregular Migration to Italy: Cause or Effect?" *Journal of Ethnic and Migration Studies* 24, no. 2: 313–32.

———. 2003. "Immigration and the Underground Economy in Receiving South European Countries: Manifold Negative Effects, Manifold Deep-Rooted Causes." *International Review of Sociology* 13, no. 1: 117–43.

———. 2004a. "Immigrants in a Segmented and Often Undeclared Labour Market." *Journal of Modern Italian Studies* 9, no. 1: 71–93.

———. 2004b. "Educational and Occupational Pathways of Migrants in Italy." *Journal of Ethnic and Migration Studies* 30, no. 6: 1145–62.

Rothenberg, Daniel. 1998. *With These Hands: The Hidden World of Migrant Farmworkers Today.* Berkeley, CA: University of California Press.

Sacco, Don Beniamino. 2002. *Le ragioni della vita: Frammenti di vita vissuta.* Vittoria: author.

Sands, Jennifer. 2002. "Europe in the Age of Globalisation: A Hotbed of Organised Crime?" *Newsletter OC* (September). members.lycos.co.uk/ocnewsletter/SGOC/sands.html (accessed December 2, 2002).

Schmitter-Heisler, Barbara. 1998. "Contexts of Immigrant Incorporation: Locating Dimensions of Opportunity and Constraints in the United States and Germany." Pp. 91–106 in *Immigration, Citizenship, and the Welfare State in Germany and the United States,* ed. Hermann Kurthen, Jürgen Fijalkowski, and Gert Wagner. Stamford, CT: JAI Press.

Schneider, Jane, and Peter Schneider. 1976. *Culture and Political Economy in Western Sicily.* New York: Academic.

———. 1996. Festival of the Poor: Fertility Decline and the Ideology of Class in Sicily, 1860–1980. Tucson, AZ: University of Arizona Press.

———. 2003. Reversible Destiny: Mafia, Antimafia, and the Struggle for Palermo. Berkeley, CA: University of California Press.

Scidà, Giuseppe, and Gabriele Pollini. 1993. *Stranieri in città: Politiche sociali e modelli d'integrazione.* Milan: FrancoAngeli.

Scillieri, Bartolo. 2000. "La presenza degli immigrati in Sicilia e in provincia di Ragusa: Evoluzione e situazione attuale." *Pagine del sud* 3, October.

Sciortino, Guiseppe. 1999. "Planning in the Dark: The Evolution of Italian Immigration Control." Pp. 233–59 in *Mechanisms of Immigration Control,* ed. Grete Brochmann and Tomas Hammar. Oxford and New York: Berg.

Solé, Carlota, and Sònia Parella. 2003. "The Labour Market and Discrimination in Spain." *Journal of Ethnic and Migration Studies* 39, no. 1: 121–40.

Stolcke, Verena. 1995. "Talking Culture: New Boundaries, New Rhetorics of Exclusion in Europe." *Current Anthropology* 36, no. 1: 1–24.

Tacoli, Cecilia. 1999. "International Migration and the Restructuring of Gender Asymmetries: Continuity and Change among Filipino Labor Migrants in Rome." *International Migration Review* 33, no. 3: 658–72.

Temin, Miriam, Friday Okonofua, Francesca Omorodion, Elisha Renne, Paul Coplan, H. Kris Heggenhougen, and Joan Kaufman. 1999. "Perceptions of

Sexual Behavior and Knowledge about Sexually Transmitted Diseases among Adolescents in Benin City, Nigeria." *International Family Planning Perspectives* 25, no. 4: 186–90, 195.

Transcrime-University of Trento. 2002. *Italy: National Report*. Trento: Transcrime.

Urban Audit. Directorate-General for Regional Policy at the European Commission. europa.eu.int/comm/regional_policy/urban2/urban/auditsrc/intro .html (accessed March 2003).

Van der Geest, Sjaak, Anke Mul, and Hans Vermeulen. 2004. "Linkages between Migration and the Care of Older People: Observations from Greece, Ghana, and the Netherlands." *Ageing and Society* 24: 431–50.

Van Dijk, Rijk. 2001. "'Voodoo' on the Doorstep: Young Nigerian Prostitutes and Magic Policing in the Netherlands." *Africa* 71, no. 4: 558–86.

Vanwesenbeeck, Ine. 2001. "Another Decade of Social Scientific Work on Sex Work: A Review of Research 1990–2000." *Annual Review of Sex Research* 12: 242–89.

Wallman, Sandra. 2001. "Global Threats, Local Options, Personal Risk: Dimensions of Migrant Sex Work in Europe." *Health, Risk & Society* 3, no. 1: 75–87.

Weitzer, Ronald, ed. 2000a. *Sex for Sale: Prostitution, Pornography, and the Sex Industry*. New York and London: Routledge.

———. 2000b. "Why We Need More Research on Sex Work." Pp. 1–13 in *Sex for Sale: Prostitution, Pornography, and the Sex Industry*, ed. Ronald Weitzer. New York and London: Routledge.

Wells, Rosemary. 1996. *Strawberry Fields: Politics, Class, and Work in California Agriculture*. Ithaca, NY: Cornell University Press.

White, Gregory. 1999. "Encouraging Unwanted Immigration." *Third World Quarterly* 20, no. 4: 839–55.

Wijers, Marjan. 1998. "Women, Labor, and Migration: The Position of Trafficked Women and Strategies for Support." Pp. 69–78 in *Global Sex Workers*, ed. Kamala Kempadoo and Jo Doezema. New York and London: Routledge.

Wolf, Eric. 1982. *Europe and the People without History*. Berkeley: University of California Press.

Zincone, Giovanna, ed. 2001. *Secondo rapporto sull'integrazione degli immigrati in Italia*. Bologna: Il Mulino.

Zontini, Elisabetta. 2002. "Female Domestic Labour Migrants and Local Politics in Bologna: The Story of a Filipino Woman." Pp. 159–76 in *The Politics of Recognizing Difference: Multiculturalism Italian Style*, ed. Ralph Grillo and Jeff Pratt. Aldershot: Ashgate.

Index

mobility of immigrants, 1, 3–4, 26–28,
42, 53–54, 58–61, 69, 77–80, 90,
99–100, 107, 113, 115, 121, 130,
143–44, 146
Moroccans, 17, 28, 50, 76
Mul, Anke, 46

Naselli, Don, 39
networks, 5–6, 11, 22, 26, 40–41, 49–52,
55, 60–61, 67–68, 77–78, 98, 107, 128,
130, 133, 141–44
Nigeria, 122–24, 131
Nigerian prostitutes: after the debt,
119, 127–28, 130, 133; enter
Palermo, 112–14; in Italy, 110–12;
legal status, 111–12, 128, 131–32;
living and working conditions,
115–17; relations with clients,
114–17, 128; relations with police,
113, 115–16, 121, 125–29; relations
with Project personnel, 117–19,
121–22, 128–30, 132–33. *See also*
Nigerian system of trafficking; sex
work
Nigerian system of trafficking:
changes in, 121, 131–32; debt
peonage and violence, 115, 119–122;
description of, 107, 109, 114–15, 133;
family and network, 122–24, 128;
supernatural threats, 120–21,
124–26, 129
Northern League, 111, 146

OHCHR (United Nations Office of the
High Commissioner for Human
Rights), 108
Okojie, Christiana, 123
OSCE (Organization for Security and
Co-operation in Europe), 108

Palermo, 17, 37–38
Poles, 76, 79, 98
police. *See* Nigerian prostitutes;
Nigerian system of trafficking; sex
work
Portes, Alejandro, 5–6
prima accoglienza, 88

Prina, Francesco, 124
Project, The, 118–19, 125–26, 128–130,
132–33
Pugliese, Enrico, 11

race and racism, 3, 11, 23, 49–52, 96,
145. *See also* domestic sector;
stereotypes of immigrants
Ragusa province, 18, 22, 67–68, 70
research methods and sites, 2, 4–6,
26–29, 108, 146
Rumbaut, Rubén, 5–6

Sacco, Don Beniamino, 77, 86
Salesian order, 38–39
Salvadorans, 44
Santa Chiara, 3, 24, 42
Santa Croce Camerina, 67, 71, 74, 76
Schneider, Jane and Peter, 36
Scillieri, Bartolo, 86, 95
Sciortino, Giuseppe, 14
section 18, 112, 117–18, 121, 128–30,
133
sex work: demand, 12, 110, 117, 130,
132–34, 143; in Europe, 109–110,
130–33; in Italy, 109–112; legal
status of, 111–13, 128; in Palermo,
107–108, 112–13; and police, 110–11,
131; Sicilians in, 112–13. *See also*
Nigerian prostitutes, Nigerian
system of trafficking
Sicilian families, 36–38, 40–41, 45,
61–62
Siegel, Dina, 129
Sri Lankans, 17–18, 20, 23, 33, 41–43,
49, 51, 60
stereotypes of immigrants, 3–4, 10–11,
14, 23–25, 48–52, 77, 79, 82, 85,
87–89, 91–92, 98, 110–11, 114,
145–46. *See also* domestic sector;
Islam; race and racism; Tunisians

Taccani, Patrizia, 61
trafficking, 100, 108–109, 112, 132–33;
in the Netherlands, 124–25. *See also*
anti-trafficking; the Project; section
18

162   *Index*

Trapani province, 17–18, 22, 27
Tunisians: enter southeast Sicily,
   76–79; family formation, 67–68,
   91–97, 99; gender, 88, 91–94,
   96–97; intermarriage with
   Sicilians, 88; living conditions,
   82–85; male world, 89–91; in
   Mazara del Vallo, 17–18; in
   Palermo, 50–52, 60, 113; relations
   with Sicilians, 82–89, 98–99;
   relations with Tunisia, 77–78, 80,
   86, 90, 142. *See also,* greenhouse
   sector; immigrant families;
   Mazara del Vallo; mobility of
   immigrants; stereotypes of
   immigrants

UIL (Unione Italiana del Lavoro), 81
UNICRI (United Nations Interregional
   Crime and Justice Research
   Institute), 122, 131
United Nations Office of the High
   Commissioner for Human Rights.
   See OHCHR

Van der Geest, Sjaak, 46
Van Dijk, Rijk, 124–25
Vermeulen, Hans, 46
Vittoria, 67, 71, 74, 76, 90

Wijers, Marjan, 133

Zaitich, Damián, 129

About the Authors

Jeffrey E. Cole is associate professor of anthropology at Dowling College in Oakdale, Long Island.

Sally S. Booth is cultural history teacher at The Ross School in East Hampton, New York.